EIGHT
GREAT WAYS
TO
HONOR
YOUR

HUSBAND

MARILYNN CHADWICK

HARVEST HOUSE PUBLISHERS
EUGENE, OREGON

EIGHT GREAT WAYS™ TO HONOR YOUR HUSBAND

Copyright © 2016 Marilynn Chadwick
Published by Harvest House Publishers
Eugene, Oregon 97402
www.harvesthousepublishers.com

Library of Congress Cataloging-in-Publication Data
    Chadwick, Marilynn.
    Eight great ways to honor your husband / Marilynn Chadwick.
       pages cm
    ISBN 978-0-7369-6727-3 (pbk.)
    ISBN 978-0-7369-6728-0 (eBook)
    1. Wives—Religious life. 2. Marriage--Religious aspects—Christianity. I. Title.
    BV4528.15.C425 2016
    248.8'435—dc23

                                2015030505

Printed in the United States of America

16 17 18 19 20 21 22 23 24 / VP-JC / 10 9 8 7 6 5 4 3 2 1

To Mom and Dad:

*I've been inspired by your stories of our family's heritage—
thanks for leaving us such a wonderful legacy of honor.
And for honoring each other through more than
six decades of marriage.*

To David:

*Honoring you is not hard—you're truly an honorable man.
You're even better than my "prayer list" of what I hoped for
in a husband. We've shared great adventures and
big dreams together—I'm thankful to be your wife.*

To Bethany, David, and Michael:

*I believe each of you is a world changer.
Every possible career path seemed pale compared to
the privilege and honor of being your mom.
You were worth my best energy—I'm so proud of you.*

Contents

Whatever Happened to Honor?

My new friend began our conversation quite innocently by asking me to pray for her marriage. We were both young wives adjusting to life in a new city. I didn't know her very well, but over the next few minutes, I would learn way more than I wanted to know about her personal life. And about her husband. She launched into a litany of all the ways he had disappointed her. She then proceeded to describe in detail how far short he fell in her eyes as a man. Before too many minutes had passed, this poor guy began to fall short in my eyes as well.

Many years have come and gone since that conversation. So why do I still remember it so well? Well, for one thing, I never could quite look at that guy in the same way again. His reputation, at least from my end, had been damaged by his wife's words. I made a mental note to myself to never, ever talk so casually to someone else about my husband's shortcomings. And I tried not to be on the receiving end of that kind of toxic spill again.

Now please don't get me wrong. It's not that David and I don't have our own flaws or that we've never struggled in our marriage. We're human too. Marriage is hard work and forces us to come to grips with our sin and selfishness like nothing else. No doubt, there are times in life when it may be appropriate to share your marriage struggles with a good friend or a wise counselor. But it was the disrespectful picture that my friend had painted of her husband that felt so wrong. So dishonoring.

And because this is a book about honor, I've been taking a long, hard look at the whole concept of honor and its importance in marriage and in our culture in general. The word *honor* describes the value or worth we give to someone because of his or her good quality or character. Honor conveys dignity, honesty, and integrity. To honor someone is to treat that person "with admiration and respect."[1]

But honor feels loftier to me than respect. Weightier. It goes deeper and has to do with intangibles like virtue and morality. Courage and self-sacrifice. Even nobility. We may not know exactly how to describe honor. But like love, we know it when we see it.

And we know when honor is missing. In some cultures around the world, to be disrespected or dishonored is so insulting that it's grounds for fighting. Some even justify the use of violence to defend one's honor or the honor of one's family. What started out as an urban slang expression for *disrespect*, "dis," has become so common as to transcend culture or age. Most any child can tell you what it means to dis somebody, or worse yet, to be dissed.

Sadly, we live in a time when dishonor is so common that it feels almost normal. Over the years, I've noticed that honor, especially in marriage, seems to be disappearing. More than once I've overheard a group of wives criticizing their husbands to each other. Sort of a group-gripe fest. And why not? It's open season on men these days. You don't have to watch television or movies too long before you see an example of "man bashing." I find this trend disturbing.

Maybe it's because I live with a servant-hearted husband who is not only the love of my life, but also my best friend. Perhaps it's because I have two grown sons and a son-in-law, all of whom are honorable young men. Or maybe it's because I grew up with a wonderful dad who has been a faithful husband and father for more than 63 years. For whatever reason, I'm bothered by how trendy it has become over the years to dis men, especially husbands and fathers. Seems like we've gotten too cool to appreciate the good guys anymore.

I pointed this out in a recent editorial I wrote for our local newspaper after the passing of the legendary University of North Carolina basketball coach Dean Smith. Along with great basketball, Coach Smith taught his players, including my husband, much about honor. David says that next to his own father, Smith was the most significant man in his life.[2] Though the excerpt below is primarily about men as fathers, it begs the question as to why the lack of honor toward men today:

> Good dads these days are hard to find. Just watch any television show. Dads are spoofed, maligned, caricatured, and generally disrespected. The message? It's just not cool to be a dad. If the same treatment were given to moms, you'd spark a revolt.
>
> But that's the nature of dads. The good ones don't whine. They don't show off. They put the needs of their families ahead of their own. And as Coach Smith modeled for us all, good dads embody self-sacrifice. In short, good dads are that reservoir of safety and unconditional love for which all kids hunger. Quite likely, they're a major factor in determining the outcome of a young person's life. The statistics aren't pretty. Girls and boys without dads are more likely to end up pregnant out of wedlock, in prison, poor, or dead. And bad dads may be worse than no dads, leaving scars inside and outside that can last a lifetime.
>
> But I'm seeing a resurgence of dad-hunger out there. I think people today are literally dying for good dads. Perhaps Coach Smith's legacy will inspire dads to be better.

Smith knew it wasn't simply about winning and losing but rather "how you play the game." His life reminds us that good guys are very cool. And just maybe, more guys will want to become good dads. Lord knows we need them.[3]

The responses to my editorial surprised me. Had I touched a nerve? Handwritten notes and emails poured in from a variety of readers—male and female, black and white, young and old. A prominent defense attorney shared memories of his own father, now deceased, reminiscing about what an honorable man his dad was in his eyes. A federal judge, a bank president, the local head of a government agency, a former mayor. Each told me about the honorable men in their lives. One even confided his heart's desire to be a man of honor within his own family. Several young moms, all who happened to be at home with small children, wrote in to praise their husbands for their hard work and for being such good husbands and fathers. Others posted on social media that they were challenged by my reminder to simply be thankful for the honorable men in their lives.

The responses made me wonder. What has happened to honor these days? Are we a culture that's thirsty for honor?

Perhaps it's because honor is sorely lacking in many of our homes. Marriages are breaking up at an alarming rate. Sadly, the percentage of wives leaving their husbands has risen dramatically. So I feel a book on honor is timely.

We'd do well to first remind ourselves that at its core, honor is a biblical concept, woven throughout the pages of Scripture to characterize our relationship with God and with each other. The Bible defines honor in the most precious of terms, conveying not only value and respect, but also extreme costliness. It's sometimes used interchangeably with the word for *wealth*. So to honor someone is to treat that person as having the utmost worth.

As I set out to write this book, it dawned on me that I could use a refresher course myself in how to show my husband how special he is to me. You'd think that after nearly four decades of marriage, I'd have this one down. David and I have had a wonderful life together. We love and respect each other and we enjoy spending time together. We've always remained faithful to one another.

But I admit that every now and then, I've been guilty of taking my husband for granted. Maybe you have done the same too. The mystery and the wonder of marriage—we can let it slide past us if we're not watching. We can forget to be thankful when the familiar becomes comfortable. To honor our husbands means to recapture a little of the awe.

And so, as part of this process, I'll be exploring ways to become more mindful about how to honor my husband. I will share some of the practical ways I've learned to communicate to David that I truly do honor him as the most special person in my life. I'll also include some valuable tips from friends in my life. Women I've admired, in part, for the ways they have honored their husbands. Some of these friends have strong, long-lasting marriages. Others have vibrant, healthy, youthful ones.

We'll walk through the pages of Scripture to explore what it has to say to us as wives who want strong marriages. What practical lessons does the Bible have to teach us about how we can honor our husbands? Plus, I'll share eight ways you can begin to honor your husband and create a culture of honor in your home.

My husband's father, the late Dr. Howard Chadwick, used to tell David, "The best gift you can give your children is a strong marriage." And so I remind those of you who are moms: The best gift you can give your children is to love and honor your husband.

Our husbands are not merely an afterthought sandwiched in between life with kids, chores, workouts, and activities. We need to be strong, faithful, and above all, intentional if we want our marriages not just to survive but to thrive. Our marriages are worth it. So are our husbands.

It's time to have an honest conversation about honor. Why does it seem to be in such short supply these days? The culture around us is groaning, desperately in need of honor. My hope is that together, we could spark a movement of honor that will spill over into a hurting and broken world. It's hard work, but the rewards are worth it. I hope you'll join me for this journey.

1

First, Become Strong

I GLANCED AT THE young couple seated at the table next to us. They were to be married the following afternoon, and this was their rehearsal dinner celebration. It sounds cliché, but there was a glow about them. That unmistakable look of being madly in love. As long-time friends of the bride's parents, we had watched her grow from a tiny baby into a lovely young woman. We were gathered with other friends and family at the charming riverside restaurant to toast the happy couple with well wishes before their big day. The exquisite meal served by candlelight under an elegant, billowy white tent was perfection. The balmy spring breeze made us all want to linger outside and enjoy the last few hours together to share memories, the usual marriage tips, and a few stories before the young man and woman began their new life together as husband and wife.

It was a familiar scene for us. David has performed hundreds of weddings in our 35-plus years of ministry at the same church. And still, we marvel at the magic of marriage. The holiness. The sheer audacity of two young people taking vows to love one another forever. Solemn promises to stick together no matter what. To be faithful until death. The enormity of it all is a bit staggering. And though divorce statistics loom heavy, young couples continue to dive into marriage with high hopes of wedded bliss and dreams of happily ever after.

The festivities carried on long into the night. Heartfelt reminiscing gave way to a few mildly embarrassing stories about the groom-to-be in more carefree days. But one theme rang true. A transformation had occurred in the young man as a result of his relationship with his soon-to-be bride. Love can do that to a man.

A buddy from his college days stood up and shared one final story about the groom's crazy antics and wild oats sown. Then he paused, as if perplexed by the changes he'd observed in his friend. "I don't really know why," he said with near-reverence, "but this girl is different. She is *solid.*" He seemed mystified as to how the changes could have happened almost overnight. "She has brought out the best in my friend," he added. "And because of her, he's becoming the man he was meant to be." Then he made a comment that still sticks out in my mind. "I guess you could say she's his *rock.*"

THE SECRET TO A GOOD MARRIAGE

The groom's young friend was more of a beer-drinking buddy than a theologian. Yet there was a strong biblical truth in his words. An honorable woman can help inspire a man to be his best. To become worthy of honor. And in that way, she is his "rock." A friend of ours who recruits for a large company agrees. "I'll hire a single woman over a single man right out of college any day," explaining that she is often more responsible, mature, and serious about her work than her male counterpart. "But just let that young man get married and have a mortgage. Suddenly his responsibility, drive, and maturity jump through the roof." The groom's buddy was right. The love of a woman, marriage, and family can help grow a guy into a man in a hurry. They can also spur him on to live a life of honor.

Honor is a noble concept. It includes attributes like dignity, value, and worth. To honor someone is to regard that person as being special.

Honor is the central theme of this book. More specifically, we'll take a look at what it means to honor our husbands and why honor is crucial to a marriage. I hope you'll begin to appreciate the unique privilege you have as a wife to inspire and empower your husband to reach his God-given potential.

Together, we'll explore what the Bible has to say about honor and why it can strengthen our marriages. Along the way, we'll look at some real-life examples of women I've known who I think have done a good job of honoring their husbands. Finally, I'll talk about some of the practical ways I've learned to honor David through our years together. Marriage is probably the best laboratory available to us for learning how to treat another person with love, respect, and honor.

But first, I have to confess the irony that I am even writing this book in the first place. In college, I was an agnostic with somewhat feminist leanings. Growing up, I'd been curious about God and attended church with my family. But I had an independent streak and wanted to live life my own way. So at around age 15, I pretty much invited God out of my life. And by the time I got to college, I had stopped believing in God altogether.

So church attendance was a habit I easily abandoned once I entered the large university. I was quickly caught up in the fun of making new friends and stretching my wings. Plus, I thrived in the exciting intellectual environment and had big dreams for my life. It didn't take long for the secular academic climate and the social whirl to sweep away any remaining spiritual leanings.

I was home from college one weekend to visit my family and reluctantly agreed to attend church with them that Sunday. I can still vividly remember my rather cynical attitude as the minister launched into what I thought was a boring sermon. I looked at the earnest young fellow and said to myself, *I can't imagine a bigger waste of a person's time and talents than being a preacher. Except being a preacher's wife.*[1] I'm sure God laughed. For a short time later, I would meet a handsome young preacher on a blind date. We would fall in love. That young preacher would become my husband barely a year after I had surrendered my own life to Christ, following a dramatic encounter with God which I will share more about later.

I wish I could tell you that my transformation was immediate. But my grasp of marriage from God's perspective did not happen right away. It took time, trial and error, and a study of the Bible, along with the help of some good role models, for God to open my eyes to His beautiful and somewhat mysterious plan for marriage.

But this book is about honor, not about how to fulfill your role in marriage, although I will spend some time on that subject in later chapters. Many good books are devoted to the biblical roles of husbands and wives. I'm not sure I can add much more to the conversation. And to be honest, I've grown a bit weary of the debates about her role versus his role in marriage, as if one size fits all. When it comes to honoring our husbands, we need to understand that no two marriages or men are exactly alike. So words or actions that make my husband feel honored and respected might go right over the head of your husband.

As I've studied what the Bible has to say about honor, and as I have become more intentional about honoring my husband, I've come face-to-face with an important realization. Honoring my husband demands way more from me than mere submission. Please understand. I'm not anti-submission with regard to the biblical framework of love and respect. It's just that to truly honor my husband, I have to set the bar much higher.

Honor requires self-sacrifice and humility. It challenges me to bridle not just my words, but my thoughts as well. It makes me bite my tongue. Honor confronts me with my sin. Honor, even more than submission, is an imposing benchmark. It's a sublimely powerful target. For if I take aim and hit the bulls-eye of honor, I am probably covering all the other virtues that make for a good marriage. Finally, if I want to honor David, I have to become honorable myself. So honor conforms me to the image of Christ. In short, honor requires a strong walk with the Lord. To truly honor my husband, I must first become strong.

God Created Us to Be Strong

To explore the concept of honor from a biblical point of view, it helps to go back to the very beginning. The first mention of marriage in the Bible is between Adam and Eve in the book of Genesis. If you want to understand God's blueprint for marriage, or anything else for that matter, it helps to look through the lens of what theologians call "original intent." What did God originally intend for marriage to look like before the fall?

In Scripture, we see that God's purpose for creating marriage was to provide companionship. Everything which God had made up to that point was good. But when He looked at Adam, He said, "It is not good for the man to be alone." Something was missing. The Genesis account explains that there was no "suitable helper" for Adam, so God plans His next step: "I will make a helper suitable for him." God goes to work to create a woman from the very stuff of man, his same substance: "So the Lord God caused the man to fall into a deep sleep; and while he was sleeping, he took one of the man's ribs and then closed up the place with flesh. Then the Lord God made a woman from the rib he had taken out of the man, and he brought her to the man" (Genesis 2:18,20-22).

A Rock of Support

The marriage relationship was God's gift to the humans. Eve was Adams's companion, but the Bible also calls her his *helper*. The exact meaning of the word *helper* has been the source of much confusion and debate for centuries. That's not surprising when you see how this word evolved into its watered-down version in our English language. Our word for *help* can mean anything from roadside assistance, to a distress call, to domestic servants.

But in Hebrew, the original language of the Old Testament, the word *help* is surprisingly strong. Help, or *ezer*, means "to support." But it goes much deeper than just assistance. One Hebrew scholar has pointed out that the word for *ezer* is actually a combination of two roots meaning "to rescue, to save," and "to be strong." In its more than 20 uses in the Old Testament, the word *ezer* is used just twice to refer to the woman. The rest of the time *ezer* refers to God doing the helping, often during battle situations.

In the Psalms, when David said, "The LORD is with me; he is my helper, I look in triumph on my enemies," he used the word *ezer* (Psalm 118:7). We also see *ezer* in the context of God running to provide aid or support to His people during times of trouble. "So do not fear, for I am with you; do not be dismayed, for I am your God. I will strengthen you and help you; I will uphold you with my righteous right hand" (Isaiah 41:10).

The word *ezer* is also closely related to the Hebrew word translated "rock," or *eben*. Thus, the *Ebenezer* stone mentioned in the Bible is a "stone of support." The prophet Ezra's name means "help" and also comes from *ezer*. Do you see the strong imagery here? Think about what it means to be strong like a rock for our husbands, our families, and those around us.

I've discovered that an important part of being a wife to a strong husband like David is to be his rock of support when everything around him feels like it is crashing down. When you grasp what it means to be a support, you begin to get an image of your role as being more like that of a rock than a doormat. Your challenge is to become strong so that you are a source of strength for a husband who will sometimes be weak.

Let's revisit the wedding rehearsal dinner described earlier in this chapter. As we've explored the beautiful biblical concept of *ezer*, we can now see why the young bridegroom's buddy I mentioned earlier was surprisingly right on target when he described the bride-to-be as his friend's "rock." Right out of the starting gate in the book of Genesis, the Bible paints a picture of the woman's ability to be a rock of support for her husband.

A Different Kind of Strength

It's clear throughout Scripture that *helper* is a strong word. But just what kind of strength are we talking about here? What does it really mean for me to be an *ezer*, or a rock, for my husband? Clearly it can't mean I am to be his physical protector. For despite all the female superheroes kicking guys into oblivion on the movie screen, the fact remains: Physically, most men are still stronger than women. Check out the USA Olympic trial standards for athletes. Men can run faster, lift more weight, put down better times in swimming. Testosterone has its place in the world.

I recently read an article boasting about all the ways women are "stronger than men." Women tend to live longer, it stated, be more stoic when sick, and now boast a higher college graduation rate than men. But I grow tired of such gender-war comparisons. Men and women are created by God to uniquely represent His complete image. "Male and female He made them," and with good reason. All scientific research aside, men and women are supposed to be *different*.

But back to our conversation about *ezer*. I'm wondering if God had in mind a more subtle kind of protector role that women bring to the marriage. I recently learned a fascinating aspect of the word *ezer* that may give us a clue. In the ancient Hebrew language, the letters were actually pictures that evolved into the modern letters used today. According to one scholar, the ancient picture letters for *ezer* were an eye, a man, and a weapon. Could it be that woman as *ezer* might function as a kind of an early warning system for her husband?

Ezer then becomes a mighty helper and protector for her husband, one who is able to reveal his enemy in times of danger, thus helping to strengthen and protect the marriage.[2] Perhaps this is why Satan targeted Eve instead of Adam. If he took the woman down, he also removed some of her husband's protection.

IF YOU WANT TO BE STRONG, BE HUMBLE

Sometimes I have noticed that I'm alert to problems or problem people before David picks up the cues. (He shares at length about this intuitive sense—which most women seem to possess—in his book for husbands, *Eight Great Ways to Honor Your Wife*.) I used to think my job was to insist that David listen to me. But I learned over the years that sometimes my discernment was not right. So if something sets off my alarm bell, I commit to praying about it before I say anything to David. "Pray it before I say it" has become my mantra, and has often prevented me from speaking too soon. But if and when I finally share the burden that's on my heart, I am able to give the right information in the right time and in the right way.

Which brings me to the importance of humility as an aspect of our role as *ezer*. The Bible consistently reminds us that strength, like honor, comes through humility. By way of servanthood. As believers and as husbands and wives, we're called to give up our rights and die to self. When I accepted Jesus, I gave Him all of me. It was the same with God's Word. Scripture was my newly found authority. I realized I couldn't stand firm on the promises and power in God's Word if I wasn't also willing to submit to its authority in my life. I'm not a halfway person by nature. Remember, I had gone from practically being an atheist to following hard after God. So when I died to myself and accepted Jesus, I instinctively knew to obey God. No looking back.

Bottom line? If I truly want to be strong in the Lord and live out what it means to be a rock, or an *ezer*, in my marriage, I must also be humble. So I want to spend some time reflecting on the delicate balance in the Bible between strength and humility.

We hear a lot about humility, but it seems it's the virtue nobody really wants. We admire it when we see it in others. But it's so against our nature to walk in humility that most of us run the other way. I once read a quote that said something like this: "Truly great people are always humble. Arrogance is the consolation prize for those who aren't at the top." Some of the most outstanding and honorable people I've met are also humble. Humility is a virtue I greatly admire, one that I tried to teach our children as they were growing up.

I'll share a little secret with you. The main reason I accepted a blind date with the man who became my husband was because of a single sentence spoken by a friend who knew David. Donna and I had gone to high school together, but had lost touch since graduating from college. She had known David when he was the college minister of her church group near Atlanta. She told me what a great guy he was. How he'd played basketball for Dean Smith at the University of North Carolina, and then had a career playing in the European professional league in Belgium and France. She went on and on and on about all of his accomplishments. But then she paused for a minute and said the words that grabbed my heart. "For all the things he's accomplished, David is incredibly humble." Humility and honor. That combination intrigued me and made me want to find out more about this guy.

The Bible is clear about the connection between humility and honor. We're reminded that "humility comes before honor" (Proverbs 18:12). "Humble yourselves before the Lord, and he will lift you up," comes the strong admonition in James 4:10. The Greek understanding of humbling ourselves in this verse literally means "to be made low." Another version adds weight to this promise: "He will lift you up, He will give you purpose" (James 4:10 AMP).

A friend of mine who seems quite confident expressed his understanding of humility this way: "Without Christ, I am an incredibly insecure person, and so I stick close to Him." Isn't that what humility really is? Apart from Christ, I'm weak and I know it. So I'm going to make a point of sticking close to Him. To abide. Jesus made it clear that abiding in Him is the secret to our strength. "I am the vine; you are the branches. Whoever abides in me and I in him, he it is that bears much fruit, for apart from me you can do nothing" (John 15:5 ESV).

If You Want to Be Strong, Abide

I was recently asked by a young mom if there was anything I'd do differently if I were just starting out in my marriage again. It didn't take me long to respond that I would simply be even more intentional about abiding in Christ. As I've learned, it's the only secret to strength in marriage that truly lasts.

David and I are both intrigued by this concept of honor in marriage. We understand how important it is that husbands and wives learn to love and honor each other. Plus, we've grown to appreciate the often-overlooked aspect of a woman's strength as the *ezer* in her marriage.

David made a comment the other day that got me to thinking. Maybe this whole thing of being strong in the Lord is even more important to expressing honor than I'd realized. "I really like it that you are not needy," he told me. What he appreciates so much, he went on to add, is that I'm not looking to him for my identity. In other words, he knows I don't expect him to meet my need for meaning or purpose. "Because of your relationship with the Lord, you come to our marriage with a full cup," he explained. "I know you're not going to drain me dry."

I've thought further about his comment and why it made me

pause. For one thing, David knows my weaknesses better than any-one. He has walked me through more fears and more tears than I can count. And yet he still considers me strong. He must see a strength in me that I don't even see in myself. Maybe abiding in Christ brings a strength that I cannot see. Abiding is not some magic pill you swal-low and then—bam, you're in! No, it's a daily process lived out by putting one foot in front of the other. Even on days when I don't feel like it. Especially when I don't feel like it. So in a sense, the call to be an *ezer* in my marriage is a call to walk daily with Christ. It's saying yes to Jesus' calling to me to be His disciple.

Perhaps as wives we'd do well to take the message of Genesis 2:18 to heart. God knew what He was doing when He created woman as *ezer*. Marriage is the closest, most intimate relationship we know on earth. We're called to love and honor each other for our entire life, to depend upon and draw strength from each other. But God also knew that ultimately, we would receive that strength through our relation-ship with Christ. He, not our spouse, is the center of our life. It's only through that kind of strength that I can be an *ezer* in my marriage. It's by being strong like a rock in the Lord that I can best honor my husband.

2

Believe the Best

FOR A GIRL WHO once said she'd never marry a minister, I changed my mind pretty quickly after I met David. I was intrigued by this kind-hearted basketball player turned preacher. He was tall and handsome, had a good sense of humor, and even sounded like the seventies icon James Taylor when he sang and played the guitar. Plus, after playing professional basketball in France for a couple of years, he was fluent in French. It was easy to fall in love with him.

But one thing worried me. David was very nice and had a sensitive nature. I can be a bit strong-willed at times and secretly wondered if I'd end up dominating him. That is, until I saw him on the volleyball court. He played on a city league team, and I went to watch him one afternoon on my way home from work. The game got very exciting and the score was close. All of a sudden, the fierce competitor in David emerged. The ball was tipped to him near the net. He jumped up and spiked the ball onto the opponent's court with incredible power. Turns out this nice guy was also a force to be reckoned with. His team went on to win the game that afternoon. And I felt pretty sure that I would not be able to push him around.

David's intensity on the volleyball court gave clues about his strength as a leader. After we got married, I saw this same strength

translate into his fierce love for our family and his passion for ministry. I have appreciated and respected his calling on both counts and
deeply admire who he is as a person. I'm grateful for his strong faith,
his character, and his integrity.

I think most women truly desire to respect their husbands. And
most men want to be honored and respected by their wives. So why
do we as women sometimes become controlling, or worse yet, critical of our husbands? Even when we wrestle to have our own way,
most of us don't really want to win the upper hand in the relationship.

Perhaps you've struggled with this tension in your marriage. I
think we'd agree that honor in the marriage relationship is a good
thing. And deep down inside, we instinctively know that it just plain
feels right to respect our husbands—to believe the best about them.
After all, as we saw earlier in Genesis 2:18, God created us to be our
husband's helper, or *ezer*, a source of rock-like strength and support.
But we can also use that *ezer* strength to work against our husband,
robbing him of strength and confidence.

I've wondered why so many marriages today are struggling. Could
one reason be that we've forgotten the importance of respecting our
husbands? Perhaps this lack of honor in marriages could be at the
core of many divorces. That's why it's important for us to explore
ways we can honor our husbands by believing the best about them.

But honor doesn't just happen. It goes against the grain of our culture. Disrespect, on the other hand, takes very little energy. It's the
path of least resistance. Honor is a narrow road. It requires strength
and intentionality. It's an important part of any strong marriage.

The Bible speaks plainly about God's design for the husband to
be the spiritual leader in the home, a concept we'll explore further in
chapter 3. But Scripture also makes it clear that men and women are
called to honor each other. I once heard a bit of common-sense wisdom about marriage that went something like this: "Don't be afraid
to be the one who loves the most." The same could be said of honor.

Don't be afraid to be the one who honors the most. Dare to take the first step by honoring your husband even before he honors you. I keep learning the same biblical principle over and over: God blesses us when we give away the very thing we desire. Or, as someone once said, "If you have a need, sow a seed." I believe you'll discover that when you give honor to your husband, you'll get it back abundantly in ways that may surprise you.

THE DANGERS OF DISHONOR

But before we get more specific about how to honor our husbands, let's talk further about dishonor. To dishonor or "dis" someone is to treat that person with disrespect. To shame or belittle them. Dishonor damages one's reputation and causes a loss of respect from others. It brings humiliation. So there's a public element of dishonor that's especially painful. Just ask anyone who's ever been bullied.

Sadly, dishonor is becoming more and more common these days in families. I'm especially troubled when I see parents allowing their young children to treat them disrespectfully in public. Seeds of disrespect sown during childhood can set the tone for dishonor in the teen years.

Sometimes I wonder if we're just too busy and moving too fast to remember to show honor to each other. The frantic pace of life impacts the way we treat our weak, our sick, and our elderly. Dishonor is tolerated, even encouraged in our media. I've already shared my concern that men, and especially dads, are the brunt of much disrespectful humor in television programming. When this becomes the new normal in our families, we can grow numb, often unaware of when we are dishonoring each other.

The Bible reminds us wives of the importance of treating our husbands with honor and respect: "A virtuous and excellent wife [worthy of honor] is the crown of her husband, but she who shames him [with her foolishness] is like rottenness in his bones" (Proverbs

12:4 AMP). Another version of this same verse tells us that a "strong woman is a crown to her husband," but a "disgraceful woman is like rot in his bones."[1] We can choose to be an *ezer*, a strong woman who gives strength and honor to her husband. Or we can be a "disgraceful" one who makes her husband ashamed. What woman in her right mind would want to be like rot in her husband's bones? Surely we are better than that.

I've wondered if a lack of respect could be one cause for the growing trend for wives to leave their husbands. In her probing article on the subject, Christine Wicker explores some reasons women are leaving their marriages. She points out that many women regard husbands as no longer essential to the family. She quotes a divorced mother of two who said this: "I realized my husband was of no added value." Wicker challenges us to get the "full chill" of that statement by imagining a husband who had divorced his wife saying the same thing.[2]

"A lot of midlife women in my acquaintance are leaving what appear to be perfectly good and loving husbands. Or thinking about it. Or cheating on them. Or wanting to. Or staying married and faithful but buying their own houses, which they either live in or keep as a bolt hole." Wicker adds, "This astonishes me. I decided one recent morning to list women I knew who fit the profile. In fifteen minutes, I came up with thirty names."[3]

Like Wicker, I have my own list of women I know who have left "perfectly good and loving" husbands. God has called us to be a strong support, an *ezer*, for our husbands. Perhaps it's time for us to learn how to stand against the enemy of our soul, who tempts women to destroy families by turning the *ezer* against their husbands.

IT MATTERS WHAT YOU THINK

Honor may be best expressed through words and deeds, but it begins in the mind. It greatly matters what we think about our husbands. What I think about David determines whether my words and actions will honor him. What we believe about our husbands can make or break our marriages.

Over the years, I've noticed a common theme in the marriages I've grown to admire. The spouses seem to be intentional about interpreting each other in a positive light. The wives speak about their husbands with respect. The husbands find ways to honor their wives. It's clear they treasure and appreciate their partner. In short, they believe the best about each other and it shows.

What's at the Core of the Most Successful Marriages?

Turns out there's some research to back up this observation. Author and longtime Gallup poll associate Marcus Buckingham surveyed thousands of married couples to discover the traits at the core of good marriages. He found something intriguing. The common thread running through happy marriages was this: In the most successful marriages, each partner rated the other person higher than that person rated him or herself.[4]

I take this to mean that as a wife, it's important for me to value and respect David, believing in him even more than he believes in himself. This got me to thinking. I can choose how and what I think about my husband. Do I respect him? Appreciate him? Do I focus on his strengths and downplay his weaknesses? Do I take time to reflect on the many ways he sacrifices for our family? Am I there for him to support and strengthen him, especially when he feels weak? In short, do I believe the best about him?

We're Accountable for Our Thoughts

Let me say it again. We get to *choose* what we think about our husbands. Or about anybody else, for that matter. Does this surprise you? Many people believe they have no responsibility for their thought life.

But the Bible is clear: "As [a man] thinks in his heart, so is he" (Proverbs 23:7 AMP). Jesus said it a different way, pointing out that sins like adultery and murder actually begin in our thought life.[5] We're accountable to God for what we think. As David's mom would say, "You can't stop the birds from flying over your head, but you can stop them from building a nest."

Thoughts influence our feelings, attitudes, and actions. No wonder they're so important. It makes sense, then, that honor begins with our mind. If we're intentional about giving honor to our husbands, or anyone else, we need to take an honest look at what we're thinking. Sometimes people try to solve problems in their marriage by fixing their feelings, only to find out this doesn't work. Feelings aren't right or wrong. Feelings are simply responders to what's going on in our mind—command central. It matters what we think.

The understanding that honor begins in our thought life takes us back to our earlier discussion in chapter 1. If we want to build a good marriage with honor at the core, we must first become strong. The Bible encourages us to be strong in the Lord. *Ezer* strong. We grow into our role as *ezer* when we abide in Christ and become strong through a close relationship with Him. We also need to be alert and watch what goes on in our mind. We must be ready to resist the devil's attacks. This reminds me of my all-time favorite verse on spiritual warfare: "Submit yourselves, then, to God. Resist the devil, and he will flee from you" (James 4:7). Notice it doesn't tell me how many times I have to resist the devil before he relents. Daily, sometimes hourly.

Dear friend, if we're serious about learning to honor our husbands, it's crucial that we're aware of the battle not only for our minds, but also for our marriages. It's time we admitted that good marriages don't come without a fight. So be ready. Suit up daily. Be strong in the Lord. Become the *ezer* for your husband. The good news is that as we submit to God and resist the devil, he will flee.

So Guard Your Mind

I don't know about you, but my mind can travel quickly to unhealthy places if I'm not careful. Especially when it comes to worrying about the people I love. I've talked to enough women over the years to know I'm not alone. Recently, I have had several conversations with young women who are struggling with fear. They're afraid of Ebola, ISIS, the turbulent economy, the future their children will face. Some live in perpetual anxiety and have had to seek counseling to help resolve their fears.

Be Alert to the Real Enemy

No doubt, fear is a very real problem today. But I wish we were as concerned about the threat that's even more insidious and more dangerous to our well-being—the breakdown of the family.

Among other things, the devil is a distractor. He's intent upon getting our minds off the real war at hand. Make no mistake about it: The war on marriage weakens our entire culture's spiritual and mental health. Failed marriages are a major factor contributing to a variety of social issues such as poverty, crime, addiction, and teen pregnancy.

Strong marriages bring health to both individuals and society. And honor, in my opinion, is one of the best safeguards against a broken marriage. There's no shortage of research to support the importance of marriage to the overall health of any culture. But all statistics aside, it's been my observation over nearly four decades of working with families that happy marriages make for happy people, and especially happy kids. When we decide to become more intentional about honoring our husbands, we're taking an important step toward building a strong marriage and guarding ourselves against the battle for our family.

It helps to take a look at how dishonor springs up in a marriage in the first place. As I've mentioned, dishonor starts in our minds.

Have you ever heard that sinister little accusatory whisper? *Why does he always do that? Why didn't he think about this? How could he be so insensitive? Wish he were more like my friend's husband.* Apparently you're not alone. Several women have confided to me that they are caught off guard by these little fiery darts, seemingly out of nowhere. The accusations sometimes become more serious. *I don't trust him. He's not capable of leading, so I'd better take control and fix things. I don't really need him to survive. I want out.*

Dishonor can be subtle because you have an enemy who has access to your mind and does his work in secret. Your friends don't live in your mind and can't know if you're struggling unless you tell them. You may not even be aware that you're dishonoring your husband with your thoughts.

The Bible reminds repeatedly of the power of our thought life. For example, "As [a man] thinks in his heart, so is he" (Proverbs 23:7 NKJV). I would add my own little addendum: "As a woman thinks of her husband, so becomes her marriage." Left unchecked, the thoughts we choose to think about our husbands can eventually make their way into our heart. And if accompanied by bitterness, jealousy, unforgiveness, and other toxic emotions, in time, they erode away like acid at our marriage.

I find it intriguing that in the Bible, one of the names for Satan is the devil, or *diabalos* in the original Greek text. It means "the divider." His other name, *Satanas*, means "the accuser." His job description is to divide relationships, families, marriages, and even nations. He's also called "the accuser of our brothers and sisters" (Revelation 12:10), so it makes sense that he would be busy at work in our minds, accusing our husbands to us and us to our husbands, "day and night" as the Bible warns. Just knowing this can help us become more alert to his schemes and more prepared to ward them off.

My longtime friend and prayer partner Beth has a strong and happy marriage. She and her husband, Gene, have raised five sons.

Beth is intentional about her walk with the Lord, her prayer life, and her marriage. She's a true *ezer* in every sense of the word. I asked her how she honored her husband. She gave me a list of tips, and one in particular stood out. Beth said she quickly dismisses any disparaging thoughts or criticisms of Gene that come into her mind. She's alert to push back the darkness when it threatens to divide them. Married more than forty years and mom to five strong football players, Beth smiled and pointed out that the thing to remember in marriage is that it's like football—the secret to winning is the *guard.*

Beth and I have learned over the years that having a prayer partner is another powerful way to place a guard around our families. I'll talk more about that later, but for now, let's remember to take seriously the power of prayer to help us guard both our minds and our marriages.

Our marriages grow stronger when we honor our husbands by believing the best about them. And by being intentional to guard our minds, as Beth pointed out, we can protect ourselves from random thoughts—negative seeds that seem harmless in the beginning but can end up as destructive thought patterns and eventually harmful words and actions.

What Happens in Your Mind Affects Your Behavior

I want to pause here to acknowledge that marriage is hard work. A strong marriage calls for courage and honesty. I don't mean to imply that we can simply sweep every problem away with a dose of positive thinking. And not every issue we face in marriage is the result of a spiritual attack. At times, we have to deal with tough situations that require painful conversations, maybe even conflict. But I want to reassure you—conflict can occur even in a good marriage. David's dad used to say that the closer two people get, the more they bump. Conflict avoidance can sometimes be a symptom of a lack of intimacy in marriage. However, there are ways to work through marital conflict without dishonoring the other person. Even when we bump heads, we need to remember to guard our minds. Especially in marriage, it's important to fight fair.

Throughout the Bible, the words translated "mind" and "heart" are often used interchangeably. Scripture takes seriously the impact our mind has on our behavior. "Above all else, guard your heart," we're warned, "for everything you do flows from it" (Proverbs 4:23). God's Word encourages us to resist destructive thoughts like worry and fear. "Don't worry about anything; instead, pray about everything," we're reminded. "Tell God what you need, and thank him for all he has done. Then you will experience God's peace, which exceeds anything we can understand. His peace will guard your hearts and minds as you live in Christ Jesus" (Philippians 4:6-7 NLT).

The word translated "guard" means to "keep watch" and is the same kind of term that would be used to describe a military guard. The implication is that a healthy thought life, combined with prayer and thanksgiving, helps you to guard your mind against outside attacks. I would add that it also helps you guard your marriage. In life and in marriage, it's clear that your thought life has great power. But don't miss the last verse, which promises that you're not alone in this battle. God's own peace will "guard your hearts and minds as you live in Christ Jesus." This reinforces our earlier discussion about how to best honor our husbands, which is to first become strong ourselves—strong in the Lord.

Practice Gratitude

Some words stand out in my mind long after other words fade away. I'll never forget the comments made by a Vietnam War veteran who told his story to a Midwestern newspaper reporter. Bob Biscan had always dreamed of being a pro baseball player. As a 19-year-old, the standout high school pitcher got his wish when he was drafted by the Cleveland Indians. Sadly, after about a year with the Indians, he was released from the organization. He later went on to play for the San Francisco Giants, but the pitcher suffered a career-ending arm injury. Biscan was then drafted into combat duty in Vietnam as an infantryman in the US Army. "I went from throwing baseballs to throwing grenades," he said.

Because of Biscan's earlier injury, his hopes of playing pro baseball were forever shattered. While in Vietnam, the young soldier saw plenty of fighting. After his tour of duty, he finally made it back home safely to American soil. Overwhelmed with relief and gratitude, he bent down and kissed the ground. "I vowed that I was never going to have another bad day as long as I lived."[6] Seems like this noble veteran made good on his promise and chooses to have good days, one after another, energized by a thankful heart.

Being rescued from a desperate condition can do that to a person. It increases the fires of gratitude like nothing else. Just ask anyone who has ever received a husband alive back from war. Or been healed of cancer. Or spared in a car wreck. The close calls of life often cause thanksgiving, relief, and love to swell large in our heart. If only we could be as grateful for the blessings of everyday life in our marriages and not just when spared from catastrophe.

Our good friend John Kasay doesn't wait for a crisis to express his appreciation for his wife, Laura. As the longtime placekicker for the Carolina Panthers, John was well-known as an effective leader on and off the football field. He's also a follower of Jesus and a deeply devoted husband and father. When he and Laura shared the speaking platform with us at a large marriage event recently, John talked about how thankful he was for Laura. He happened to mention that he actually made a list of the things he loves about her. A gratitude list? Not something you'd normally expect from a tough-as-nails former NFL record holder.

I happen to know firsthand that John practices what he preaches. Several years ago, we were both walking out of a parents' meeting at our kids' school when he made an offhand comment about his wife: "Laura is the most resourceful person I know." Such an ordinary comment, but it stuck in my mind. Why do I remember it years later? Simply this: I knew Laura was beautiful, charming, funny, and a great mom. What I did not know was that she was also resourceful—that she manages people and resources well and is a good problem solver. That's something only John could have pointed out. And he's right. I began to notice Laura's resourcefulness and picked her to be part of a select team of volunteers who oversee an inner-city scholarship program in our community. Not only is John thankful for Laura; he believes the best about her and honors her by verbalizing this to others. When we show gratitude for our spouses, especially in front of others, our words carry more weight than we realize.

You might find it helpful to make your own gratitude list of the things you love about your husband. Give yourself some time. Journal prayerfully. Be specific. Ask God to help you remember all the reasons you fell in love with him in the first place. Or maybe you'd rather write down a few things to be thankful for each day and reflect on those. A wise friend and mentor combines this exercise with prayer for her husband each morning as a regular part of her daily quiet time. Be creative. Simple gestures like a gratitude list can help you develop a mindset of thankfulness. Who knows? Maybe you'll have an opportunity to mention one specific thing you're thankful for about your husband to someone else. You never know the positive impact your gratitude may have on someone else's marriage.

If you're looking for some practical, biblical training tips on how to build up your "gratitude muscles," I'd suggest you read the short New Testament book of Philippians. Filled with lots of encouragement, Philippians is sometimes called the "epistle of joy." That's interesting, considering that Paul was in prison and soon to be executed when he penned the short letter.

Even in the midst of suffering, Paul found countless ways to express his gratitude to God and itemized what I like to imagine as an outline for his own gratitude list: "Finally, brothers, whatever is true, whatever is honorable, whatever is just, whatever is pure, whatever is lovely, whatever is commendable, if there is any excellence, if there is anything worthy of praise, think about these things" (Philippians 4:8 ESV). Or as another version puts it, "Let your mind dwell on these things."[7] The word "think" in the original Greek text is *logizomai* and can be translated "to think upon or ponder." It can also mean "to count, calculate, or enumerate."[8] Sounds like a list to me. Again, why not count the things you are most thankful for in your husband? Write them down. Reflect on them. Let your mind "dwell on these things."

Paul followed up with these powerful words: "What you have learned and received and heard and seen in me—practice these things, and the God of peace will be with you" (Philippians 4:9 ESV). Paul sounds like a personal trainer challenging us to practice gratitude. Practice is part of life, whether it's in sports, piano, computer skills, or learning a foreign language. If you want to get better at something, you naturally have to practice. So why not practice gratitude? It's one of the best ways I know to create a healthy thought life. Practicing gratitude can help you to believe the best about your husband. This, in turn, will honor him and strengthen your marriage.

Remember, we get to choose what we believe about our husbands. Let's choose to believe the best.

What I love

① He's self-less.
- He always puts my needs & my happiness before his own

② He's honest
- Even when given the opportunity to lie, he decides to be truthful, regardless of consequences.

③ He's all-in.
- Whatever he does, whether its work, love, ministry, sports, etc.. he does it with all his heart

④ He doesn't let things fester
- If there's a problem or hes upset about something, he handles it immediately. He doesn't wait

3

Build Him Up

FOR THE WOMAN WHO ended up becoming one of my all-time favorite friends and mentors, Mom Harper and I got off to a rocky start. The feisty, retired schoolteacher worked with the college ministry David had started while he was in seminary. Alice and her husband, Forrest, or "Mom and Dad Harper" as everyone called them, had boundless energy and enthusiasm. They were part of the adult team of volunteers who poured life into what had become a thriving ministry to students.

Mom and Dad Harper's only child, a son, had died as a small boy. Many years later, though the couple had no children of their own, they were like an extra set of parents to the college kids who flocked to the church every Sunday night.

Soon after we began dating, David introduced me to the college group. The scrutiny I felt as the outsider who was dating their beloved pastor was a bit daunting at first. But pretty soon, the college kids warmed up to me. I had just gotten out of college myself, and was a beginner in my spiritual journey. So this lively group, the "Westminster Fellowship" as they called themselves, helped me grow in my newfound faith. A short time later, when David and I got engaged, everyone was so happy for us. Everyone, that is, except Mom Harper.

I'll never forget the night. We had just finished dinner when David decided to share our good news. After he told everyone we were engaged to be married, Mom Harper got up abruptly and left the table. She didn't smile, didn't say a word. Ouch. I could only guess the reasons for her reaction. I'm sure I didn't look the part of the future wife she'd envisioned for her favorite young minister. In fact, I looked exactly like what I was—a former university sorority girl now working in the big-city corporate world. Besides, I had only recently stopped running from God and was definitely a rookie to the world of church ministry. I'm sure Mom Harper wondered if I could provide the strength and support David would need in his role as a minister.

Though my faith at that time was raw, it was very real. About a year earlier, I'd had a life-changing encounter with God while reading C.S. Lewis's *Mere Christianity*, the gripping account of his own journey from atheist to believer. From the very beginning, David said he could always see my heart for the Lord. He was never even one bit worried about how I'd fill the role of minister's wife.

In time, Mom Harper's attitude toward me began to thaw. I think she could tell that I truly loved David and supported his calling. I would pepper her with questions about life, about ministry, and about this young preacher she knew so well. Ever the teacher, she took me under her wing and became my friend. Smart, headstrong, and a real truth-teller, Mom Harper was just what I needed. Dad Harper was warm and friendly—a little laid back with a dry wit. He didn't have quite the same feisty personality as his wife, but I noticed how Mom Harper respected him. She knew how to build him up. Her example as a strong woman who was also a "rock of support" for her husband made an impression on me.

Our friendship continued to grow, and when David and I got married, Mom Harper gave us a special wedding gift—her treasured collection of antique French prints. David and I headed off to serve our first church in Texas, and Mom Harper continued to encourage me through her letters, always laced with words of wisdom and lots of humor. Our correspondence lasted for years until she died in her late eighties.

Looking back, I think Mom Harper was a lot like the older woman mentioned in Titus 2 who encouraged the younger women to grow in their faith and to love their husbands.[1] She had grasped the concept of mentoring before it had become popular. Perhaps Mom Harper invested in me because she could tell I was eager to learn. Maybe she saw that I would help David face the many challenges that come with the ministry. After all, I was a fighter—and just maybe I was a little bit like Mom Harper. I'd like to think she saw some *ezer* in me.

Let Him Lead

My friend Carol was educated as an attorney, but chose to pour most of her energy into raising her five now-grown kids. She's a smart, gifted leader, and has lots of common sense. After years of friendship, Carol is one whose advice I treasure. I know I can always count on my plainspoken friend to get right to the point.

One night over dinner, I casually mentioned to her that I was writing a book about how wives can honor their husbands. Then I asked how she honored her husband. I was taken aback by her answer. She simply said, "I let him lead." There was not a trace of a whine. "He does a really good job as a leader," she added. "That is what the Bible teaches, right?" She didn't even bother to overexplain her point. Now I know Carol well enough to know that hers is a marriage of equals, with a lot of give and take, mutuality, and freedom. She and her husband share family decisions and responsibilities. But she's learned to respect his God-given role as the spiritual leader of their family.

As I talked with more women about this topic, I was intrigued to notice that the stronger the woman's confidence in her own leadership ability, the easier she seemed to grasp the importance of building up her husband's leadership. A friend who oversees a large counseling department put it well: "I'm not really threatened by my husband's spiritual leadership—it's kind of like the military. There's a chain of command." Her marriage, too, is one I would describe as a marriage of equals. I'm wondering if women who are strong leaders themselves instinctively grasp God's design for marital teamwork and harmony.

Are You Willing to Be Led?

It makes sense that if I want my husband to be a leader, I should try to actually let him lead, right? Sounds so simple, but hard to put into practice. It's much easier to take control. But if I truly desire for David to be a *good* leader, then naturally I will want to find ways to build him up and to help him lead well. How I do that doesn't matter so much as that I do it.

I've noticed that women today like to celebrate and develop their own giftedness as leaders. That's a good thing. But we can sometimes be resistant when it comes to responding to our husband's spiritual leadership in our families. I'm not insensitive to the struggle. Remember, I was the girl who was a spiritual skeptic with feminist leanings before I became a Christian.

I have to confess that in some ways, becoming a follower of Jesus was remarkably uncomplicated for me. After years of rejecting the faith, the hard part had been the struggle leading up to my surrender. But when I finally made the choice to give my entire life to Christ, there was no holding back. I realized that my life, as I knew it, was no longer my own. Like I always say, when you surrender to Christ, if it doesn't feel a little like dying, you probably didn't do it.

One of the first major changes that occurred is that instead of regarding the Bible as some outdated book, I understood it to be God's Word. I believed it was the truth, and it became my blueprint for living. So if the Bible said I was to put others before myself, that's what I intended to do. Be generous with my money? No problem. Fight for justice? Absolutely. Submit to my husband's spiritual leadership in marriage? Well, that one sure sounded out of step with the world, but I would give it my best shot. After all, these were God's words. He had invented marriage in the first place, so I figured He knew how to best make it work.

The Bible opens its discussion on spiritual leadership in marriage by reminding us to first "submit to one another out of reverence for Christ" (Ephesians 5:21). Then comes a special word for wives: "Wives, submit yourselves to your own husbands as you do to the Lord." Husbands are then commanded to "love [their] wives, just as Christ loved the church and gave himself up for her" (Ephesians 5:22, 25). Let's think about that for a minute. Our husbands are called to love us so much they're willing to die for us—a sacrificial servant-leadership that comes at great cost. Looks to me like they got the tougher job description.[2]

I especially like this interpretation:

> Wives, understand and support your husbands in ways that show your support for Christ. The husband provides leadership to his wife the way Christ does to his church, not by domineering but by cherishing. So just as the church submits to Christ as he exercises such leadership, wives should likewise submit to their husbands (Ephesians 5:22-24 MSG).

In What Ways Are You and Your Husband a Good Fit?

I'm sure we would agree that every husband is different. What supports my husband and builds him up may not help yours at all. And of course every wife is different. So the kind of help and strength you give to your husband will depend on your own gifts and personality.

To help us explore ways to do just that, let's take another look at the creation narrative and our original calling to be the helper, or the *ezer* in our marriages: "Now the LORD God said, 'It is not good (beneficial) for the man to be alone; I will make him a helper [one who balances him—a counterpart who is] suitable and complementary for him'" (Genesis 2:18 AMP). Notice that the wife is to be a helper who is *complementary* for her husband. Obviously, our femaleness complements our husband's maleness.

But I like to think that our unique wiring also complements our own husband's wiring, making us well-suited not just to be a helper, but to be *his* helper. Another version translates the same verse this way: "It is not good that the man should be alone; I will make him a helper *fit* for him" (Genesis 2:18 ESV). Notice the use of the word "fit." How encouraging to think that God created you to be a good *fit* for your husband. And him to be a good fit for you.

David and I have discovered over our years of marriage that our gifts complement each other. He appreciates my gifts of teaching and encouragement and is patient in the areas that don't come so easily for me—such as keeping a perfectly organized home. I'd like to think that God selected me as the *ezer* that David specifically needed for his personality and calling.

And I challenge you to consider that God handpicked you, with your own unique gifts and personality, to be just the *ezer* that will best complement your husband. That gives a new twist to the old expression "a match made in heaven."

SPEAK WORDS OF LIFE

Did you know that women talk more than men? It's a proven fact. We actually talk a lot more, beginning from when we're just children. The average woman speaks about 20,000 words each day to a man's 7000, or nearly three times as many.[3] So if we want to use our words to honor our husbands, we certainly have no shortage of building blocks.

I've discovered that one of the most powerful ways to build up my husband is with my words—both the words I speak *to* him and the worlds I speak *about* him. Careless words can easily tarnish his reputation in the eyes of others. As wives, we sometimes forget the weight our words carry.

Proverbs 14:1 reminds us that "the wise woman builds her house," but a foolish one "tears hers down." In the Bible, the term translated "house" is often synonymous with "family." So when we build up our husbands, we are also strengthening our family, our "house." Let's take a look at what the Bible says about the power of our words, and explore practical ways to put words to work for us as we honor our husbands.

The Bible talks about two kinds of words—words of life and words of death. It repeatedly cautions us about the dangers of the tongue. Our words have great power for good or evil—we should pause here to consider that God holds us accountable for the words we speak. Think about it: Families and friendships are broken apart by words. Wars are started with words. Our tongue "sets the whole course of one's life on fire, and is itself set on fire by hell" according to James 3:6. In short, we're warned that "death and life are in the power of the tongue" (Proverbs 18:21 kjv).

So it naturally follows that our words would be some of our most powerful tools for building up or tearing down our marriages. With our words, we honor our husbands by building them up. We give life and encouragement. Or, our words can bring death and discouragement.

Words We Speak About Our Husbands

As a newlywed, I remember noticing the ways women talked about their husbands in public. Some spoke as though their husbands could do no wrong, while others talked with reckless abandon about the poor guys that could apparently do no right. The odd thing is that there was not *that* much difference that I could see in the men themselves...it was their wives' perceptions of their husbands that caught my attention and seemed to make the difference.

We sometimes forget the power of our words and their impact on how others see our husbands. To honor our husbands with the words we speak *about* them is to treat them with respect—to make them shine. But sometimes, even when we don't mean to, we can lower another person's opinion of our husbands with our careless words. To hurt anyone's reputation is a serious offense. Even our courts recognize the danger of *slander*, referring to it in legal terminology as "the action or crime of making a false spoken statement damaging to a person's reputation."[4] How much more mindful we should be to guard our husband's good name.

One of my wise young friends with a strong marriage put it well: "I try to compliment my husband in front of others when he is present, but also when he is absent. In situations where it is tempting to criticize publicly, I try to say nothing and follow up on the conversation when we are in home in private. Then I honor him by choosing my words wisely—prayerfully most of the time!"

The Bible speaks to the seriousness of harming someone's reputation, warning us "to slander no one, to be peaceable and considerate, and always to be gentle toward everyone" (Titus 3:2). The word translated "slander" is the Greek term *blasphemeo*. It comes from two words—*blapto,* which means "to injure," and *pheme*, or "speech." It can be translated "to hurt another's reputation through slur or insult."[5]

The Anglicized version, or blasphemy, is most often used to describe the offense of speaking out against God. But it also applies to speaking against others. "It is from within, out of a person's heart, that evil thoughts come—sexual immorality, theft, murder, adultery, greed, malice, deceit, lewdness, envy, slander, arrogance and folly" (Mark 7:21-22). It's kind of sobering to see slander right up there with what we might consider "more serious" offenses. Makes me think twice when I'm tempted to gossip.

Half the battle in our commitment to build up our husbands is simply to be aware—to become more intentional about speaking words of life. Both *to* our husbands and *about* them. In the marriages I've admired most over the years, the wives seem to instinctively know how to strengthen and support their husbands, aware that their words can have a positive impact on how the husband sees himself and how others see him.

Words We Speak to Our Husbands

My friend Susie is a woman who knows how to use her words well. She's intelligent, talented, beautiful, and fun to be around. It's no wonder. Susie's an encourager who instinctively knows how to make anyone feel special. She also understands what it means to honor her husband.

Over the years, I've noticed how Susie's eyes light up whenever she sees Bob. I've listened to the words she speaks to him and about him to others. She treats him as though he's very special to her, and without even knowing it, she makes him shine. I once happened to mention to Susie that I really liked the way she treated her husband. She thought for a minute and then commented, "I'm always careful about the words I speak. So much damage can be done by our words. I'm always telling the younger girls to watch how they talk to their husbands. Once spoken, words can't ever be taken back."

Perhaps we'd be more careful if we knew the full impact of our words. We learned earlier about the importance of guarding our minds. We would be wise to place a similar emphasis on guarding our words. The Bible encourages us to do just that: "Set a guard over my mouth, LORD; keep watch over the door of my lips" (Psalm 141:3).

From time to time, I do a little exercise which I call a "word fast." I simply avoid speaking negative or critical words to or about anyone for an entire day. Not as easy as it sounds. A word fast causes me to carefully watch not only what comes out of my mouth, but also the thoughts that give birth to those words. I've learned that guarding my tongue is no small matter. My friend Laura also tries to watch her words and devised her own somewhat humorous method of self-control. She laughed the other day as she confided that sometimes she actually bites her tongue as a reminder to keep her mouth shut. Whatever works for you, do it.

But just as a wife's careless or negative words can injure her husband's reputation, her positive and encouraging words can have a great impact on how others see him. This is especially true in our families. I've noticed how words I speak to our children about David can influence what they think about their dad. Recently for Father's Day, I asked each of our three grown kids to write a few sentences to their dad listing what they were thankful for about him. Easy enough. Then I printed their comments on a page and stuck it in his Father's Day card along with our gift to him. David got so caught up reading what they wrote that he almost forgot to open his present. He was deeply moved by their heartfelt words. And I noticed that he still keeps the card on the table beside his favorite chair. Just a few deeply encouraging words from those we love can have a greater impact than we realize.

The words we speak directly *to* our husbands have a special ability to strengthen them. If I had known from the beginning of our marriage how my words could have such a powerful impact, I'd have been more intentional about encouraging him early on. One episode especially stands out in my mind. David and I were about a decade into our marriage and had gone through a bumpy time in the church. He was wondering about his leadership and even wrestling with his calling. Some internal staff conflicts had left him feeling weary and defeated. I didn't fully realize just how low he was at the time until he told this story several years later.

Looking back, I remember the incident well because we happened to be on vacation at the time. When I woke up one morning, David was sitting quietly on the side of the bed looking out the window over the ocean. As he tells the story, I simply put my hand on his shoulder and said, "I still believe in you." Five simple words made a difference in his ability to go on when everything in him felt like giving up. No wonder the Bible continually reminds us to "encourage one another and build each other up" (1 Thessalonians 5:11). Our words have such power. It's not only important to believe in our husbands, but from time to time we need to tell them so.

BE GENTLE

A framed Norman Rockwell print hung on one of the walls of our home for many years. I memorized virtually every detail of the picture and can still see the burly, muscled farmer cradling a tiny bird in his rough, work-worn hands with this caption underneath: "Nothing is as strong as gentleness, nothing as gentle as real strength."

Gentleness, in my opinion, is an underrated virtue in our hard-charging, competitive world. It's sometimes perceived as weakness, even a liability. Yet *gentle* is one of the few adjectives Jesus ever used to describe Himself. "I am gentle and humble in heart," He tells us. And when we come to Him, He promises we will "find rest for [our] souls" (Matthew 11:29). The word translated "gentle," *praus*, doesn't imply softness or weakness. Rather, it describes a disciplined restraint or bridled power. Think of it more like a racehorse whose power has been harnessed for speed. Or the athletes whose hours of training channel their mighty strength into competition. Gentleness is always kind. But it can also win races. It has power. It brings healing. It gives rest. And it is very strong.

The Power of Gentleness

Gentleness brings honor to our marriages. And like our words, gentleness is a powerful tool that can build up our husbands. Especially when they need comfort, or understanding, or rest. Because Jesus is gentle, we become more gentle the closer we get to Him, the more we abide. There's also a supernatural quality to gentleness—that's why we find it listed among the fruit of the Holy Spirit.[6] It's a paradox, but we actually need power in order to become truly gentle—the power that comes from the Holy Spirit.

Gentleness can be especially helpful when it comes to dealing with difficulties or conflicts. It's a powerful tool for wives who are trying to reach husbands who may be far from God. The Bible encourages wives to keep on loving and honoring their unbelieving husbands, pointing out that "even if some do not obey the word, they may be won without a word by the conduct of their wives, when they see your respectful and pure conduct." The behavior described here is characterized by "the imperishable beauty of a gentle and quiet spirit" (1 Peter 3:1-4 ESV).

As we've learned, the word translated "gentle" here is same word Jesus used to describe Himself. So if a wife is acting like Jesus in her relationship with her husband, it's no wonder that gentleness can win husbands over when words fall short.

Let's face it: There are times in marriage when our words will fail to get our point across. Perhaps your husband follows Jesus but has a blind spot to God's truth in a certain area of his life. These words from 1 Peter 3 should encourage all of us to learn how to wait. They emphasize that God's work in a husband is often accomplished "without a word" on our part. Sometimes the strongest thing we can do is to be gentle and quiet. And then to commit the matter to prayer. Like I've often said, "There are times to say it, and times to pray it."

Gentleness Works When Words Fail

When I think of what a gentle and quiet spirit looks like, I'm reminded of my friend Grace. She is elegant and refined, a lovely woman inside and out. She moves in the most influential social circles in her community and is especially known for her work in charitable activities. She is dearly loved and respected by all who know her, and especially by her husband and children. For many years, Grace's husband was a high-powered and influential business executive. Though he deeply loved his wife, he wanted little to do with the Lord. Over the years, Grace continued to love and honor her husband. I noticed the way she spoke well of him to others and built him up in front of their children.

Grace grew strong in her walk with the Lord. I watched in amazement as her husband gradually began to respond to his wife's love and respect and her "gentle and quiet spirit." In God's perfect timing, this powerhouse of a man was captivated by the Lord, largely due to the witness of his wife. The change in him was immediate. Even his teenaged daughter remarked with wonder at how her dad had changed. God had used Grace's gentle and quiet spirit not only to honor her husband, but to help open the door to eternal life.

Let's face it. Marriage takes hard work. Even good marriages can have issues that need God's help. Maybe you've tried repeatedly to get through to your husband. Perhaps he isn't listening to God about a certain area of his life. Or maybe, like Grace's husband, he's rejected God altogether. Those are the times to lean into God, pray, and entrust the problem into God's hands. This takes us back to our commitment to first be strong in Him. And as we grow in our own relationship with Jesus, we commit to gentleness.

I encourage you, like Grace did, to continue to be faithful and to let your life speak in those places where your words have come up empty. Your walk with the Lord, your joy, your answered prayers can all be part of the "winning over" of your husband. Just remember, "There are times to say it, and times to pray it." Or to put it another way, sometimes you have to "pray and walk away." Not from your husband, of course, but from trying to fix him or the problem. There are times for words, and times for no words. But it's always the right time to be gentle.

Building Him Up Also Strengthens You

We have been talking about ways to honor our husbands starting with our own walk with the Lord. We've seen that humility and gentleness should be present in all our relationships, especially in our marriages. It's important to believe the best about our husbands, to be thankful for them, and to guard our minds against thoughts that would divide us.

While God asks your husband to lead your home, He instructs you to build it (Proverbs 14:1). Think about the importance of building a home and family. The New Testament Greek word translated "build," or *oikodomeo*, means "to build, build up, rebuild; to edify, strengthen, develop another person's life through acts and words of love and encouragement." It can also be defined "to build a house, to construct; to advance a person's spiritual condition."[7]

The Bible says that when we get married, we become *one* with our husband. We are two individuals with our own unique gifts, talents, likes, dislikes, life experiences, strengths, and weakness. But mysteriously, we are also now "one flesh." So it's important to understand that when you strengthen and honor your husband, you are in some way actually building up yourself.

Becoming a Wife Who Builds

Ponder these verses:

> The wise woman builds her house, but with her own hands the foolish one tears hers down (Proverbs 14:1).

> Therefore encourage one another and build one another up, just as you are doing (1 Thessalonians 5:11 ESV).

Take another look at the New Testament Greek word translated "build," or *oikodomeo*: Reflect on the definition: "to build, to build up, rebuild; to edify, strengthen, develop another person's life through acts and words of love and encouragement." It can also be defined "to build a house, to construct; to advance a person's spiritual condition."[8]

How does this expand your understanding of what it means to build up your husband? To build your home?

Pray:

Lord, thank You for this special husband You've given to me. I pray for greater insight into ways to honor him and build him up. Help me find ways to make him shine. You know him even better than I do and created him and prepared a purpose for his life. You even gifted and equipped him especially for that purpose. I pray for his relationship with You to grow stronger each day. Give me wisdom and words to speak which will encourage him as a leader. And remind me that when he is strong, I am strong, for You have mysteriously made us one.

I also pray for grace and truth to challenge him when needed. Help me to speak the truth in love. And I pray for Your Holy Spirit to prompt me when it's time to keep quiet—those times when words do more harm than good. Remind me to first get the log out of my own eye so I can see clearly how best to be my husband's helper, his *ezer*. Make me into the kind of woman who is willing to take You at Your Word and trust You in all things—especially with my marriage.

4

Fight for Him

DEEP WITHIN THE HEART of every good woman lives a warrior. I've arrived at this conclusion after years of watching women face all manner of danger to support and protect the ones they love. Her fierce love for her family can make even the most timid woman do courageous things. And whether you're married or single, with or without children of your own, my guess is that somewhere along the way, you've learned what it means to fight for someone you love. It naturally follows that sometimes the best way you can honor your husband is to fight for him.

My friend Ange is from Rwanda. She knows what it means to fight for her husband. Gentle and soft-spoken, Ange waged a brave battle for eight years—a shining example of a woman who honored her husband by her perseverance.

Ange was in high school when the horrific Rwandan genocide broke out in 1994. She and her fiancé, Emanuel, fled on foot to a refugee camp in neighboring Congo. They were married in the camp. One day, soldiers attacked. Ange and Emanuel became separated as they fled for their lives. She searched frantically for Emanuel, hiding in the forest for weeks with no clean water, food, or shelter.

Ange made her way to Kenya with the help of a relief organization. She enrolled in Bible college and continued to search for Emanuel.

After several more years, even her closest friends tried to persuade Ange to accept that Emanuel was dead—and to remarry.

But Ange sensed the Holy Spirit whispering to her to keep on fighting and to believe that Emanuel was still alive. These words became her lifeline: "We rejoice in our sufferings, because we know that suffering produces perseverance; perseverance, character; and character hope. And hope does not disappoint us."[1]

She happened to be listening to a radio program that helped find missing family members after the war, and heard the amazing news that Emanuel was still alive. "It was like a dream!" she shared. "I stayed up all night praising and thanking God." So after eight long years, Ange and Emanuel were finally reunited—all because she would never gave up.

While your struggle may not require the same level of courage as Ange's, my guess is that you are quietly waging your own brave battles to fight for your husband. Maybe you're his rock of support as he struggles through a long illness. Or you're a military wife holding the family together while your husband is off at war. Perhaps it's a job loss that has thrown you into your *ezer* role. Or together, you and your husband are caring for a sick child, or aging parents. Perhaps you are fighting side by side with your husband to chase after a dream. One thing is for sure: There are many faces of *ezer*.

The Warrior Side of *Ezer*

Let's go back to our earlier conversation about how God created Eve to be Adam's *ezer*, his rock of support. We learned that at times, *ezer* may rescue someone from danger. That's why God is often referred to in the Old Testament as Israel's *ezer*, their helper who gives power to His people during battles. We see that *ezer* is not only her husband's helper and his rock of support, she also "has his back."

I have to admit that I'm drawn to the warrior side of *ezer*. Maybe it's because I've always had some "rescuer" in me. As a small child, I used to pin a towel around my shoulders as my cape and try to fly like Superman. I was always hoping to save someone from danger. Later, when I was six, my very understanding parents bought me a pair of PF Flyers and a toy Winchester rifle so I could fight my "battles." Even now, I have to confess that I love superhero movies. I guess I still have some rescuer in me. Maybe you do too.

Ezer *as an Early Warning System*

David appreciates this side of me. He's glad that I'm loyal and protective of him—confident that I always have his back. But the guy is 6'7" tall, a former college basketball player who went on to play in the European professional league for a few years. Obviously, he doesn't need me to physically protect him. So the *ezer*-in-me, the God-given warrior side, must be a different kind of strength. A strength built on sensitivity and discernment. A spiritual strength that draws power from my relationship with the Lord. That's the kind of strength that will best help me fulfill my role as *ezer* and best honor my husband.

As we noted earlier, some scholars have compared the role of *ezer* to that of an early warning system. That would imply that we have the ability to alert our husbands to danger. David would tell you that sometimes I read people better than he does. I tend to be alert to problems or problem people before he picks up on the cues. Perhaps it's because he's more of a big-picture thinker. And like many women, I can see the tiniest of details, the fine print. That's why David and I make a good team.

On a couple of occasions, I've alerted David to my uneasiness about someone's character or motives and prevented him from stepping into trouble. I used to think it was my job to insist that he listen to me. After all, I was warning him for his own good, right? But I've learned over the years to move gently and prayerfully, and to proceed with caution. Because sometimes my timing is not right. Or maybe I don't have all the facts. And sometimes my hunches are just plain wrong.

A rather humorous but humbling episode taught me a good lesson. We were on a missions trip to Latin America. It was soon after 9/11, and everyone was still nervous about international travel. David preached at a large gathering in a nearby city. It was late at night and we planned to drive with a local pastor back to his home. On our way to the car, two guys, seemingly out of nowhere, approached David and the pastor, wanting a ride.

David and the pastor didn't know the two rather scruffy men, but the men said they had been at the gathering. So the pastor agreed to let them ride in the back of our car. *What was he thinking?* I could hear the guys in the backseat, laughing and cutting up like two unruly middle school boys. They switched back and forth from English to Spanish. It was clear from their accents that they were from the southern part of the United States. What were they doing in this part of the world anyway? And why were they at a church gathering? They sure didn't look or act the part.

My imagination went a little crazy. Maybe these guys were criminals or renegade soldiers, planning to kill us and throw us out of the car! I kept my worries to myself as we drove back to the pastor's home. And it's a good thing. Turns out these characters were actually American missionaries serving in one of the most hostile and dangerous regions in Latin America. Lesson learned! I've come to realize that if my intuitions are born out of fear or anxiety, I'm probably off base. In fact, fear can wipe out my discernment altogether. But the fact remains, part of my role as an *ezer* and part of the way I honor my husband is to fight for him. To be alert to danger, but without being anxious.

Taking Our Job Seriously

You may be wondering why I am talking about having a warrior mentality in a book on marriage. It's because I believe we're at war. Marriages today are falling apart at an alarming rate. Some experts now say that as many as two-thirds of all divorces are initiated by wives. It's time we take seriously our job to keep watch over our marriages and our families. It's time to stay strong in our faith. Just the other day, I heard about four more broken marriages in my circle of acquaintances. Sadly, the list of casualties keeps growing.

Let's remember that we're emphasizing *honor*—something we find in short supply these days. I've discovered that honoring my husband in today's culture requires something of a fight. It should sober us to realize we have enemies. Not just enemies of our soul, but also of our marriage. We wage war on several fronts. Some of our fights are against our own selfish nature, our "flesh." Honoring our husbands can sometimes go against the grain of our flesh. So our battle for a strong marriage is a battle against our own selfish tendencies like self-centeredness, pride, disrespect, laziness, or impatience.

We also find ourselves up against a world that degrades and disrespects marriage. We're called to resist its wrong messages about marriage and even about men. I remind you of our earlier discussion about the generally disrespectful treatment of men in the popular media.

Finally, we wrestle against the spiritual forces of darkness who would seek to divide our home. The devil is an accuser and a divider who would love nothing more than to break up our marriages. The Bible tells us he "prowls around like a roaring lion looking for someone to devour" (1 Peter 5:8). Quite simply, he wants your mind and he wants your marriage. Another version of the same verse warns us to "Stay alert!" and "watch out for your great enemy, the devil" (1 Peter 5:8 NLT). We're to remain ready and prepared to fight.

It helps to realize we have our own mighty weapons that can put the devil and his minions on the run—prayer and God's Word. Remember, our enemies are defeated foes because of the overwhelming victory Jesus won on the cross. So I encourage you to fight with hope. To stand firm. We can defend ourselves and our marriages with the powerful spiritual weapons given to us by God.

We fight most effectively when we are preventive, taking steps to defend our marriage before it's in danger. Prayer puts us on the offensive. We are intentional to pray in advance. To be self-controlled, alert, and watchful. Let's resolve now to never let the devil catch us sleepwalking through our life or our marriage.

PRAY LIKE YOU MEAN IT

If you were to ask me what's the single most important thing you can do to strengthen your marriage and to honor your husband, I would simply say this: Pray for him. Pray like you mean it. Pray like you believe prayer works. Pray like you believe God works through your prayers. And make prayer for your husband a priority.

I have seen many wives' prayers empower and encourage husbands who are already following hard after Jesus. And I have seen prayer soften the hearts of men who have rejected God for years. I am a bit mystified as to why prayer works when words fall short. I just know it does.

My dear friend June prayed for years for her husband, Bryan, to accept Christ. He continued to resist the gospel. My friend was wise. She refused to nag. But she did set aside 15 minutes every morning to pray for her husband. I don't know how long she prayed for him this way. But, sometime later, I watched in amazement as Bryan walked forward to accept Christ at a Billy Graham crusade in our city. During the invitation, I happened to glance over at the aisle on my right and was startled to see this man who had stiff-armed God all those years. There he was, wife by his side, resolutely heading straight to the front of the arena, where he gave his life to Jesus Christ once and for all.

The ripple effect of that one influential man's devotion to Christ was powerful. The impact he had on many others, including his own family, can't be measured. All because of the quiet witness and faithful prayers of a strong wife. Like my husband always says, "If you don't love Jesus and you have a praying wife, or a praying mother, look out—you're toast!"

David and I have seen God work mightily through prayer during our nearly four decades of marriage. Especially when we're wrestling with an obstacle that's too big for us. Or a shared enemy. Or a fiery trial. In short, prayer helps us stay connected to Jesus. To abide in Him. And when we abide, we grow strong.

Realizing the Urgency of Prayer

Two incidents motivated me to step up my prayer life and to become more intentional about the way I prayed for David and our family, and eventually for the world. These experiences also drew us together as prayer partners. As a result, we began to be more aware of answered prayers as our relationships with Jesus and with each other grew stronger.

The first experience was a personal one, the other more global. The personal struggle David and I faced was our long battle with infertility. It was only prayer and God's grace that helped us to endure the long years of waiting before the births of our three children. It was during that time that I learned to search God's Word for wisdom and take my stand on the promises revealed in Scripture. I began to understand what Paul meant when he explained how God's power is made perfect in our weakness.[2] Also, I experienced a rather dramatic healing miracle that resulted in the births of our children. Seeing God's power at work in this way left me forever convinced that prayer is worth my best effort.

The second incident, more global in its scope, was the attack on our nation on 9/11. In the panic that followed the attacks, I experienced what I can only describe as a powerful calling by God to pray for His very broken world. He began to put various countries on my heart, so I started to experiment with a more strategic approach to prayer. I sensed Him calling me to enlarge my prayers to include specific countries by name, especially for His people who were suffering persecution.

Recognizing the Power of Prayer

Prayer became a way for David and me to "fight" for the advancement of God's kingdom, especially in places that were hostile to the gospel. Over time, we saw some rather startling answers to our prayers. We believe it was only prayer that opened doors for us, and eventually for our church, to travel all over the world. We formed partnerships with courageous workers advancing the gospel in places like India, Sudan, Burundi, Rwanda, and Lebanon, all of which had simply started out as items on our prayer list.

Of course I also continued to pray fervently for the safety of my own family, for our community, and for our nation. In the years that followed 9/11, I began to see a prayer pattern emerge, with dramatic answers to both the personal and global prayers. I share the simple prayer method I discovered, along with stories from my prayer journey, in *Sometimes He Whispers, Sometimes He Roars: Learning to Hear the Voice of God.*[3]

Some of the practical lessons I learned about prayer in the aftermath of these life experiences have had a more far-reaching impact on our family than I could have imagined. Specifically, my prayers for David are focused, more structured, and I think, more powerful. I'm mindful to ask him about areas where he needs prayer. As I pray for him more regularly, I'm more attuned to the struggles and challenges he faces. I sometimes see little problems before they became big problems. I try to find promises in God's Word which apply to his needs. And when we see specific answers to prayer, it causes us to rejoice together and to trust God even more.

I've continued to experiment with practical ways to weave prayer into my daily life. Making prayer both practical and daily are keys to powerful prayer. This kind of "prayer without ceasing" helps me to deal with my tendency to worry. Worry comes with the territory when we love people. But I've discovered that anxiety can actually make me more alert to prayer.

Paul's words to the church at Philippi have inspired me to make worry have a positive outcome: "Don't worry about anything," he encouraged them. "Instead, pray about everything" (Philippians 4:6 NLT). I'm struck by the word "instead." Paul didn't say to just stop worrying. He said instead of worrying, pray. In other words, we are encouraged to channel the energy we'd use on worry to pray.

Cultivating Specific Strategies for Prayer

This reminds me of a strategy I learned when I took karate in high school. Our instructor trained us to use the enemy's energy against him. A violent attack could be redirected to incapacitate our attacker. What better way to disarm the powers of darkness than to turn the very anxiety intended to disable us into energy for a powerful counterattack? Or as nineteenth-century preacher Charles Spurgeon challenges, "Turn your cares into prayers."[4]

As you become more intentional about praying for your husband, I imagine you'll come up with your own practical tips for how to become more focused in your prayer life. You might want to experiment with a list like I did. I pray for David and each of our children on different days of the week.[5]

Or you could use Jesus' own prayer tutorial, which is commonly known as the Lord's Prayer. Jesus Himself taught us to ask God boldly for His will to be done here on Earth, just like in heaven. Prayers for provision, confession, forgiveness, and deliverance are all included in His powerful prayer recipe.[6] Simply praying each petition of the Lord's Prayer for your husband takes about a minute. I timed it. You could even set your cell phone as a reminder to pray through these petitions for your husband for one minute each day.

I especially love the idea of having a "prayer trigger" for my husband. A prayer trigger is simply a visual reminder to pray. Whenever I see Canadian geese flying overhead, I pray for David. Geese are known for their unique "V" flying formation. The head goose at the front of the formation dares not turn his head to see if the other geese are with him, lest the force of the wind snap his neck. The other geese will persistently "honk" to let the head goose know they are behind him. David is fond of sharing this illustration about leadership and teamwork. For that reason, geese are a great prayer trigger. I naturally remember to say a quick prayer for David when I see geese flying overhead, especially when I hear them honking their affirmations to the head goose.

These are short, simple strategies. And if you are faithful to pray for your husband day after day, you'll begin to build a habit. You'll cover your husband in ongoing prayer. You'll have his back. Maybe another reason Satan wants to target us like he did Eve is to knock us out of our *ezer* role and wreck our prayers, thus removing some of our husband's front line of defense. He surely does not want us praying for our husbands, standing with them, or fighting for them.

STAND YOUR GROUND

"I'm sorry," the nurse said to me gently. "This hardly ever happens. For some reason, your hormone levels were extremely high this time...but you are not pregnant." I sat stunned. All signs had pointed to pregnancy. This time, it looked like our long wait was over. Finally, we'd hold a baby in our arms. But once again, our hopes were dashed. I was spent. Month after month and year after year of disappointment had left me raw. I felt vulnerable. Exposed. Needy. I couldn't have imagined that waiting for something I desperately wanted would be so hard. Nor could I realize then that I would eventually come to find treasures in the dark place I called barrenness.

More than 30 years have now passed. Nearly 96 months of surgeries, medications, treatments, prayer, and the eventual births of our 3 children would follow that episode. But I can honestly say that God taught me my most valuable lessons on faith during those years of what I call "wait training." I'd have to admit that both grace and grit were forged into my character. I learned to persevere. And David and I learned to lean on each other. He drew strength from my faith to keep going when his own wore down. And I drew strength from his leadership and direction when I couldn't see where to turn next.

In time, I became more resilient. I gained greater compassion for the suffering. I learned to find hope in life's barren places. And I discovered some surprising benefits of not getting what I wanted when I wanted it. Put simply, I learned how to wait well.

I've discovered that one of the best ways for me to honor David is simply to believe God's Word. Persevering faith is one of the best gifts I can give him. It's another way to support him, to be his *ezer*. To stand my ground, planted firmly on God's Word when situations may look hopeless. To endure storms. To go the distance. To agree with him in prayer. To ask him in the hard times, "How can I pray for you?" To remind him when the answers come. These are some ways we can fight the good fight. Together.

Going the Distance

Let's face it. We all have troubles. Life hurts. It's not like Jesus didn't warn us. "In this world you will have trouble. But take heart!" He reminds us. "I have overcome the world" (John 16:33). But as I've shared repeatedly, we must first stay connected to Jesus if we hope to stand our ground in the spiritual fight.

The trials of life will most certainly impact our marriage. Trouble can draw us closer or divide us. That's why the wedding vows cover things like "for better, for worse, for richer, for poorer, in sickness and in health…" And the vows are permanent. Enduring. "For as long as you both shall live."

I honor my husband by standing my ground in faithfulness to our vows. Fighting for him means not only enduring my own trials but helping him to endure his. It means I go the distance with him. Until our life on Earth is finished.

To stand one's ground can also mean to endure. The Greek word translated "endure" is *hypomeno.* It comes from two words: *hypo,* or "under," and *meno,* "to remain." *Meno* is the same word Jesus used when He told us to abide in Him (John 15:7). So to endure is to "remain under" a painful trial with grace. It's bearing up under a load of trouble with a tranquil mind. When we abide in the light, we can endure in the dark. Put another way, when the storms of life hit— and they will—we'll be better able to endure if we have been faithful to abide in Christ. We can't endure apart from Jesus.

Training Develops Perseverance

Every time the winter or summer Olympic trials draw near, various athletes around the world have the opportunity to show the results of their intense training regimens to see who will win the chance to compete for their country. As believers, we, too, should train for our trials. James 1:2 encourages us this way: "Consider it pure joy…whenever you face trials of many kinds, because you know that the testing of your faith produces perseverance."

Have you thought about how your daily routine of prayer, reading God's Word, listening, and obedience day after day after day prepares you to stand strong when faced with a trial? Training prepares you in advance to fight the fight of faith. Athletes endure the pain of training for the love of the sport.

Dear friend, do you love the fight? Paul calls the fight of faith a "good fight." It's been said that we should love the contest of faith in the same way an athlete loves his sport. Honestly, I don't know if I'd say I *love* trials. But there is something invigorating about approaching each day by strengthening myself in God's Word and being intentional about prayer. Especially for my husband and children. I should walk away from my prayer time armed and ready. Expectant and watchful. Alert to both signs of God at work and opportunities to step out in faith. Ready to share the gospel, to meet a need, to take back territory from the enemy. Prepared to stand my ground and stand on the Word of God. In doing all this I honor David.

Finishing Well

One of the best things about having decades of years of marriage under my belt is the vantage point. I can see the big picture. I've watched many marriages succeed and fail over the years. I remind you that marriage is a marathon, not a mile run. Sadly, I have seen plenty of men and women start the race well, only to cave in after 20 or even 30 years of marriage. Perhaps they never learned to abide in Christ, so when trouble hit, they couldn't endure. Or maybe they just stopped practicing what they knew to be true.

It's important to honor your husband and work to build a strong marriage when you are newlyweds. But it's also important to keep doing the right thing as you grow older. Even though our kids are grown and I've got more freedom, I continue to remind myself of the important calling to be David's wife. I'm choosing to enjoy this time with more freedom in my schedule to grow even closer to him. A good marriage is the best gift we can give our kids and grandkids.

Let me take a minute to honor those of you who have remained faithful throughout many years of marriage. Perhaps you're among those wonderful few who have made it to the 50-year mark and beyond. You know exactly what is meant by the saying, "Old age is not for sissies." Aging calls for abiding and endurance. It requires faith and sacrificial love to keep those wedding vows when circumstances have made life painful. Aging shows what you're really made of.

My own father has been a devoted husband and dad to three daughters. He's also one of the few remaining World War II submarine veterans. He and my mother have been married more than 63 years. Mom was a wonderful wife to her husband through the years— his helper and his best friend. Now I watch Daddy caring tenderly for my mother, who has been bedridden and totally dependent upon him for the last decade. I've watched him honor his wedding vows day after day. He is fighting the bravest battle of his life. He honors her, and she honors him back. Their example shines brighter than any sermon on faithfulness ever could to their children, grandchildren, and great-grandchildren.

Standing your ground in marriage is hard work. Maybe that's why we see so few examples of long-term faithfulness. Perhaps, as women, we sometimes fall short because we get caught up in other things. Perhaps we drift away from God and let go of our commitment to abide in Christ. Or maybe we drift away from our husband altogether.

Take the Pulse of Your Marriage

I was at home full-time when our children were small. But when they all went to school, I worked for a year with a group of high-powered executive women. Though several of them had troubled teenaged children, they didn't seem as worried as I would have expected, given the severity of the problems. Then it dawned on me one day. The work we did was important. Vibrant. Fast-paced. Rewarding. Perhaps even numbing. Because one thing was clear: These women did not appear to be feeling their children's pain.

I want to comment on the danger of being numb, especially as it relates to marriage. If we want to fight for our husbands, and to pray for them effectively, we must, to some degree, feel their pain. Many women live such fast-paced lives these days and are so absorbed in their work as to be numb to pain and immune to the promptings of the Holy Spirit. Too busy or too numb to pray, they are often caught unaware by life's storms. Overwork, like any other addiction, can do that to a person.

After my epiphany at work that day, I began noticing some small issues with our children. Nothing big, but I wanted to make sure I dealt with the small problems before they became big ones. I stopped working altogether for a season. It gave me time and space to evaluate. To make sure I felt the pulse of our family. To make sure I could feel their pain.

How much more should we feel the pulse in our marriages? I want to mention, again, how saddened I have been by the news of several long-term marriages that have broken up recently in my sphere of friends. And I wonder. Why didn't the early warning signals go off before the damage was done? F.B. Meyer, a Bible teacher in England, once said, "No man suddenly becomes base." Erosion doesn't happen overnight. And no marriage suddenly fails.

CALLED TO BE WORLD-CHANGERS

Let's dare to ask ourselves some hard questions. Are we too busy to read our husband's signals? To feel his pain? To feel the pulse of our family? Are we too busy to pray for them? Somewhere along the way, have we stopped standing our ground?

In summary, we've discussed the often-overlooked aspect of being our husband's helper, his *ezer*. The calling to fight for him. Primarily, that fight is in the spiritual realm, through prayer, where the fiercest of battles are fought. *Ezer* then becomes a mighty helper and protector for her husband. One who is able to discern his enemy in times of danger, thus helping to strengthen and protect the marriage.

God has made us fighters for a reason. And quite honestly, I'm convinced we're built for far more than simply fighting for our own rights. I believe we're called to be world-changers, starting with our own families. As usual, God's wisdom about serving others and giving our life away flies in the face of conventional wisdom. I would agree with a comment made by my friend Joan Wright, a highly acclaimed executive coach, speaker, and author of *UP: Pursuing Significance in Leadership and Life.*[7] Joan challenges both men and women as they pursue significance not to aim their sights on simply being the best in the world, but rather to be the best *for* the world.

I believe we as women, as *ezers,* are designed not just to be fighters but to fight *for* someone. To fight for our husbands. Then for our children, for the downtrodden, for the lost and broken of this world. We women are at our best, in my opinion, when we're serving, loving, giving, and laying down our lives for others. But, if we miss the opportunity to be our best in our homes, and especially with our husbands, we have failed to be faithful.

5

Guard Your Home

"There's no place like home. There's no place like home." Dorothy closed her eyes and repeated the words over and over while clicking the heels of her ruby red slippers. Suddenly, she began to spiral through time and space and awakened in her own bed, shaken and dazed, but utterly relieved to find herself back in Kansas. Uncle Henry and Auntie Em hover over their injured niece, worriedly wiping her brow. And no wonder. Dorothy had been hit in the head by flying debris in a fierce Midwestern tornado. Knocked unconscious, she drifted into a dreamlike adventure in the beautiful but dangerous Land of Oz.

Faced with talking trees, flying monkeys, and a fiercely wicked witch, Dorothy and her new friends, a scarecrow, a tin man, and a lion, band together and set out to find the wizard who can grant their wishes. Dorothy, who had always yearned for adventure "somewhere over the rainbow," now has but one wish—to go home. The foursome must destroy the much-feared wicked witch before their requests will be granted by the wizard. They accomplish their mission. Dorothy's wanderlust satisfied, she's forever grateful for the familiar comforts of home.

What do you think of when you hear the word *home*? Just saying or hearing the word itself makes me breathe a little easier. Home is the place where I can step out of the fast lane. Home is family. Home is comfort. Home is love.

I asked David what came to mind when he thought of our home. "It's where I'm able to rest," he said. "Home is where I'm protected." Then he thought for a moment and added more words to his list: "Recharge. Peace. Laughter." "Home's the one place I can be alone, and not feel guilty about it," he added. "It's my place to get away from the battles of the day. A place to recover so I can go back into the fight a little stronger."

With the incredibly intense demands of ministry, preaching responsibilities each week, a radio show, and the inevitable crises that come his way as the pastor of a large church, David needs a haven. I want our home to be that place he can always go to renew. The place that helps him stay strong. The place where he can laugh.

Through the years, I've watched David turn down all kinds of "bigger and better" opportunities in order to keep family front and center in his life. It's clear that after his commitment to the Lord, family comes next. So any discussion about ways to honor my husband needs to include our home and what happens in it. Home is the heartbeat of our family.

One of the most practical ways I've learned to support David is simply through the environment I create in our home. Our surroundings, daily routine, and even our health habits will either build him up or weigh him down. Even more than the physical surroundings of our home, I'm mindful of what happens here. How do we treat each other? What are our conversations about? How hectic is our schedule? What kinds of movies do we watch? When do we find time to connect? You get the point.

I'll say it again: Every husband is different and so is every home. What makes our home work for us may be different than what works for yours. David can handle some "messiness" in our surroundings, especially when we are both writing books or traveling together. Thank goodness we're able give each other grace in the "tidying up" department when we need it. But we don't give up our coffee time or day off together, no matter how busy we get. Time together is important to our home life, so we guard it fiercely. We have figured out what's important to us, and how to major on the majors.

Friend, I believe it's worth it to be creative and explore ways to make sure our home works well for the particular way our husband is wired. And it's worth the effort to guard our home against the things that would rob our peace.

KEEPER OF THE CASTLE

It's no wonder most of us have strong feelings about our homes. The concept of home is woven into the very fabric of democracy. Men and women have fought and died for the freedoms we enjoy in our homes. Even the Bill of Rights protects the safety and privacy of the home, prohibiting "unreasonable searches and seizures." Home rests upon the "inalienable rights" of "life, liberty, and the pursuit of happiness."[1]

The sanctity of the home dates back to Roman times. It was Cicero who once said, "What more sacred, what more strongly guarded by every holy feeling, than a man's own home?"[2] A well-known English proverb puts it this way: "A man's home is his castle."

The castle was the center of daily life as well as a refuge against enemies during the dark and dangerous Middle Ages. Those who could afford to defend themselves employed soldiers, constructed moats, and rigged their own security systems to guard against marauding intruders.

The interior tower of the castle was called the "keep." It was kind of like a giant "panic room," a place of safety, and the refuge of last resort should the rest of the castle fall to an enemy.[3] Once while traveling through Europe, I got a firsthand look at a castle and its keep.

Seeing the fortified tower, the keep, gave me new insight into Paul's instructions in Titus 2. Older women, he advised, were to encourage the younger women to "love their husbands, to love their children" and to be "keepers at home" (Titus 2:3-5 KJV).

It makes sense now why scholars familiar with castles in the King James era would choose "keepers at home" to translate the Greek word *oikourgos*. It comes from two words which mean "house or family" and "guard or watcher." The "keeper at home" would thus protect the family as well as manage her household.

Let's reflect on this powerful imagery for a moment. To be "keepers at home" challenges us not only to work hard at creating our home, but to carefully watch what happens there. You can see how the idea of being a keeper adds depth to our understanding of *ezer*. Remember that as *ezer*, the woman was not only her husband's helper or rock of support, but also his guard.

Ways to Guard Your Home

Now let's explore what it means to guard our home. What, exactly, do we guard against? Thankfully, we don't face the same barbaric enemies that keepers at home encountered in ancient times. We don't have to deal with marauding soldiers, pillaging bands of thieves, or bubonic plagues. Nor do we face the same kind of exposure to the elements, lack of education, starvation, or civil war that many women faced in America just a century and a half ago.

But we'd have to agree there are more subtle, stealthy intruders that threaten the peace and safety of our homes and families today. Enemies from within and without attack our families. And since these modern enemies may fly under the radar, we need to be more discerning, more watchful, and wiser than ever.

In trying to describe home as a haven for our family, the word *peace* keeps coming to my mind. I've observed how a peaceful home nourishes David's soul and renews his energy. Plus, it's beneficial to our children and to those who visit our home.

But if I want a peaceful home, I have to guard against enemies. Peace is not passive. To have peace in our home, I have to work for it. Sometimes peace doesn't come without a fight. Thomas Jefferson is reported to have said, "The price of freedom is eternal vigilance." Or to borrow a line from a famous presidential speech, "Peace, like war, must be waged."[4] Let's explore some ways to guard our homes against these seen and unseen enemies.

Replace Worry with Peace

Peace is a priority in our home. A peaceful home refreshes David and blesses our entire family. But I'll say it again. If I'm intent upon "waging peace," it helps to know my enemies. I've noticed that the quickest way to rob the peace in our home is through worry. Anxiety can drain our family's energy and quench its calm faster than just about anything. And it's contagious. When the kids were small, if I became worried, they would worry too. Worry is also exhausting. I agree with a friend who once coined this acronym for W-O-R-R-Y: "Worry Only Robs Rest from You."

There are lots of other good reasons to fight against worry. For one thing, it shows a lack of trust. Worry says loud and clear that I don't trust David, and worse yet, I don't trust God. On the other hand, when I refuse to be anxious, when I trust God and remain peaceful, I help to create a climate of peace.

Most people who know me would probably not call me an excessive worrier. I appear pretty calm on the surface. And I have done plenty of dangerous things in my life. I've visited war-torn countries and traveled on short-term missions trips to six continents. I've even learned to be comfortable speaking to large groups, a common fear for many people. But for much of my life, I wrestled with worry.

David has been very patient and encouraging over the years in helping me deal with this unseen enemy. There were times early in our marriage when fear held me quietly in its grip. Fear of storms, fear of intruders, fear of illness, fear of flying. You name it—I probably wrestled with it.

But I've learned to be ruthless with this enemy. And through God's grace, lots of prayer, and David's encouragement, I have wrestled most of my fears to the ground. I'm not completely worry-free, but I can tell you that I no longer feel like a prisoner to fear.

There are some who suffer a more extreme version of anxiety—perhaps even full-fledged panic attacks. I've seen friends and extended family members caught in its grip. If fear is like getting attacked by a lion, anxiety is like being chewed slowly to death by a poisonous coral snake. Both are deadly. Sometimes the battle is too fierce to wage alone, and a good Christian counselor can help you take steps to get at the root of the anxiety.

Sadly, women sometimes deal with anxiety through destructive behaviors like addictions, overeating, or overwork to detach themselves from the anxiety, resulting in what one psychologist calls "the most addicted, overweight, busy, numbed-out population of humans in history."[5]

For now, I'll just say that these twin invaders, fear and anxiety, can wreak havoc on a home and a marriage. God doesn't treat fear and worry as small things. He tells you to "cast all your anxiety on him" because He cares for you (1 Peter 5:7). There's a reason He commands you to "have no fear"[6] and "be anxious for nothing."[7] Like with any stubborn problem, the first step is to confront anxiety head-on and call it out for the enemy that it is.

Laugh at the Future

One of the things I love most about David is that he can get our family to laugh at the very things that cause us to worry. Once when our daughter Bethany was very young, he challenged her in a light-hearted way to conquer her "fret flies" and dared her to ride a ferris wheel for the first time.

I'm glad David's not a worrier. That doesn't mean he is unaware of dangers and problems. He just doesn't tend to chew on them or over-think imaginary scenarios. He doesn't spend energy looking back at the "if onlys" or ahead to the "what ifs."

It's not like David has never had bad things happen to him. In his twenties he was beaten and robbed in his own home while house-sitting for his parents. He's dealt with all kinds of tragedies and emergencies throughout our years of ministry. But I've seen firsthand that his faith has strengthened him. I've often told him that the greatest gift he has to give others is his faith.

He's right about one thing. It is incredibly freeing to laugh in the face of worry. And it's healthy to find a way to lighten up. However we choose to fight worry, it's important that we resist. We can learn to put that "warrior side" of our *ezer* to work in guarding our homes against worry.

I found some good tips on dealing with anxiety from the famed Proverbs 31 wife. I believe this woman had some warrior in her. I'm intrigued by the Hebrew adjective used to describe this wife and mother—*chayil*, commonly translated "virtuous" or "excellent." If we dig a little deeper, we learn that *chayil* also means "valiant" or "courageous." And like the word *ezer*, it depicts strength.

Chayil is used about 100 times in the Old Testament, most often to mean military power. When we read about King David's renowned "mighty warriors,"[8] the word *chayil* is used to describe them. So you can see that *chayil* is not a tame word.

I'm curious why a word that best describes soldiers is used in Proverbs 31 for a wife and mother whose master passion was her home and her family. Perhaps it's because she managed her home with expert leadership and skill. Or maybe it's because she built wealth for her family and expanded her trade. She was also kind and generous to the poor. All with a grace and dignity that earned the praise of her husband and children.

But I like to think *chayil* was chosen as the word to describe the Proverbs 31 woman because she was fearless. "She is clothed with strength and dignity," we're told, "and she can laugh at the days to come."[9] Another version says she "laughs without fear of the future."[10] This word translated "laugh" can also mean "to mock or scoff." So we see that this woman is not only fearless, but she has a sense of humor, and maybe even a bit of a swagger. Whatever else she is, the Proverbs 31 woman is definitely not anxious.

Her strength brought honor to her husband. He had "full confidence" in her and she brought him "good, not harm" all the days of his life (Proverbs 31:11-12). But look more closely at her secret. The reason for her confidence is revealed at the end of the chapter: "A woman who fears the LORD is to be praised" (Proverbs 31:30). Her deep faith in God was the reason she could be a rock of support to her husband. Simply stated, the Proverbs 31 woman had no fear except the fear of the Lord. Her life reminds us that the best way to honor our husbands is to "first, be strong in the Lord."

I can't say I've mastered the art of laughing at the future. But I have noticed if I can laugh at a small problem, it sets a peaceful tone in our home. I've developed my own little strategy for disarming worries. I encourage you to experiment with this method or create your own ways to resist worry.

The Three-Minute Rule

> Don't worry about anything; instead, pray about every-
> thing. Tell God what you need... (Philippians 4:6 NLT).

How many times on any given day are you tempted to worry? If you're like me, the answer is plenty. Next time a petty problem causes you to unravel, I challenge you to pause. Try to *wait for three minutes* before you allow yourself to become anxious. Time yourself if necessary, but stay calm. Just for three minutes. Then see what happens. I'm amazed at how many of life's little whirlwinds clear up in under three minutes! My kids used to call this "Mom's three-minute rule."

It's the minor irritations of life that quickly steal our joy. The "little foxes" that nibble away at our marriages. And it's the trifling annoyances that rob our daily calm.

What if we stood up to the enemy and said, "No! I will not surrender my peace of mind." I may not be able to keep my cool forever, but surely I can keep calm for three minutes. Especially if I remember to turn the matter over to God through prayer. "Cast all your anxiety on him because he cares for you," we're reminded in 1 Peter 5:7. But casting your anxieties, I've learned, takes a bit of spiritual muscle.

Daily life gives me plenty of chances to practice. The traffic light that takes forever to change when I am already late for that appointment. Lost keys. My urge to snap impatiently at my husband or children. Could I wait just three minutes before I react? And breathe a quick prayer for God's peace? So much the better.

Our children are watching to see how my husband and I navigate life's inevitable anxieties. I was reminded of this years ago when driving our youngest child across town to a birthday party. We were running late. Of course I hit every stoplight along the way, and I was getting frazzled.

Then, just as things were looking up, I got stuck at a railroad crossing with an oncoming train. I became exasperated by this ridiculously long train, and my impatience showed.

"Hey Mom," quipped my son from the back seat. "What happened to your three-minute rule?" I stopped, took a deep breath, and said, "Okay, let's time this train [Mr. Smarty Pants]." And so we did. And you know what? The train took forever, or so it seemed. But just as the caboose whooshed by, the three-minute mark passed on my dashboard clock. Exactly. Three minutes to the second.

Next time you feel tempted to worry, take a deep breath. Think. Pray. Respond, don't react. And wait three minutes. Guard your heart...and your peace. And save all that energy for the really big battles in life.

Commit to Prayer

As I've said before, praying for my husband is one of the most important ways I can honor him. I keep learning this lesson again and again. For me, the best way to make sure this happens is to start my day with a quiet time in prayer and God's Word, following a brisk half hour of exercise. My secret is to get this done before the rest of the world is up and moving. My "morning launch" is quite possibly the most powerful addition I've made to my daily routine in the last 20 years. The results are more far-reaching than I'd ever imagined.

I had always thought an early-morning quiet time with God sounded like a good idea. I'm not a morning person, but as I shared earlier, 9/11 changed my perspective about everything. I began to see prayer as my weapon against worry, a means of blessing my family, and a powerful way to impact the world. I share the details of that journey, along with tips on my morning launch, in *Sometimes He Whispers, Sometimes He Roars: Learning to Hear the Voice of God.*[11]

Earlier I mentioned how I use the energy of worry to help sharpen my prayers. Let's take another look at my pivotal verse from Philippians:

> Don't worry about anything; instead, pray about everything. Tell God what you need, and thank him for all he has done. Then you will experience God's peace, which exceeds anything we can understand. His peace will guard your hearts and minds as you live in Christ Jesus (Philippians 4:7 NLT).

Notice the end result of turning our worries into prayer. We are promised that God's peace will guard our hearts and minds. Sounds like another good weapon against anxiety, doesn't it?

I'll have to say that getting up earlier was not easy at first, but I wanted to pray more than I wanted to sleep. If I could just get my shoes on, it was downhill after that. Plus, my ever-faithful running buddy Susan had more discipline than I did. She would always be waiting at the end of her driveway in the dark. I didn't want to let her down. Positive peer pressure can be a wonderful thing.

After a 30-minute run, I'd go home to a nice cup of coffee and uninterrupted quiet to read God's Word. I had time enough to let God's powerful promises sink in and time enough to pray.

I have to confess that I'd had a tendency to wake up to dark moods or anxious thoughts. But the early run seemed to kick out the cobwebs, give me a good boost of endorphins, making me more alert. I'd keep reminding myself, *Don't evaluate your day until you run, have coffee, and pray.* Or, *I may be barely alive at five, but I will be great by eight.*

My running buddy Susan also happens to be a nurse practitioner. She tells me there are many physiological reasons for the feel-good sensation after my morning launch. We both like our routine so much that we have managed to get in a few runs each week for 15 years. This routine is so powerful at warding off anxiety that I sometimes encourage women to try something similar for 30 days to see if it gives some relief from their worries. And if you lack the discipline, like I did, find a good running buddy!

In summary, my early-morning prayer time is the best hour of my day. It's how I stay connected to God and first become strong in Him. It's when I am faithful to cover David in prayer. To be his rock of support, his spiritual *ezer*. Everything else flows out of that time of abiding. And as we've learned, abiding is connected to endurance. I'll say it again: When I am faithful to abide in the light, I am better able to endure in the dark. And better able to guard my home against unseen foes like fear and worry.

Create Structure

A while back, I was driving through Kentucky. As I crossed over the state line, I was greeted by a billboard with the slogan "Kentucky: Unbridled Spirit." At first, the thought of being unbridled sounded appealing, especially right there in the middle of horse country. But as I thought about it, being unbridled—without restraint—didn't sound like such a good thing (apologies to those of you in or from Kentucky). Humans work best with boundaries. *Unbridled* sounds too close to *disorder*. Not a good strategy in light of the subtle war that rages against our homes and families.

If wars are won through discipline, strategy, and preparation, then they're lost by disorder and lack of readiness. I'm reminded of the US Coast Guard motto *Semper Paratus*, which means "always ready." If I'm serious about guarding our home, it makes sense to look at how well it operates—and how I can best make it a peaceful haven for David.

Disorder is a stealth enemy of families. This insight came from a friend who works in a fragile community. Ken Gilliard, or Pastor Ken, as he's affectionately known, is the minister of a thriving inner-city church. He grew up one of four children born to a single mother in a poor neighborhood. Pastor Ken made his way out of poverty. But he felt called by God to return as a minister to the same community and help other families escape poverty. David and I have long admired Pastor Ken's heart to help urban families raise strong, healthy children who are able to reach their God-given potential.

One day Pastor Ken shared a rather surprising insight with me. "Do you know what families need most in poor neighborhoods?" *Hmm*, I thought to myself. *Education, jobs, health care, Jesus?* "Structure," he said emphatically. "They need structure. If they don't first have structure, they don't have anywhere to hang all the other lessons they learn." I've never forgotten Pastor Ken's answer.

Families in Pastor Ken's neighborhood face all kinds of enemies that threaten to derail their homes. So he and a team of staff and volunteers created a comprehensive after-school program to help the children with homework habits and study skills. A parent support group, called Family Fun Night, organized by my friend Yvette, provides instruction on practical topics such as how to create an orderly environment at home. Families learn to prepare healthy meals and better manage their money. Structure has provided a framework for the many changes that have occurred as people give their lives to Christ and study His Word. The results are impressive. The high school graduation rate has gone up. Some kids have attended college. Crime has gone down. The community is healthier and safer.

If Pastor Ken is correct, then structure can help not just fragile families but all families create a peaceful home. The word *structure* comes from a Latin word that means "to build." Structure emphasizes organization. So the opposite of structure is disorder, or disorganization.

I enjoy structure and order. Most people do. Even children respond better with clear boundaries in the home. But the needs of each family are different, so you will have to figure out what kind of structure works best for your marriage and your family.

Do you enjoy the actual physical care of your home? Our friends Michael and Kathleen share an incredible talent for creating a lovely home. They singlehandedly assembled every interior piece of wood in their beautiful mountain log cabin. For them, home is a work of art, a hobby, and a place of peace. They enjoy sharing their home with others. God has wired them both with similar gifts of hospitality, organization, and giving—all wrapped in a servant's heart. So their gifts flourish in their home.

David and I, on the other hand, do a lot of study and writing from home. We've had to learn to tolerate a bit of messiness at times. So in our case, I can best create a peaceful home by making the best use of David's limited time and energy.

Yard care is also not our priority. We live on a wooded side street, so nobody really minds. For years, David faithfully cut grass, raked leaves, and did his due diligence. But after a while, I decided I'd rather have time with him. So I hired a lawn service. And later, he gave me back the same grace and hired a once-a-month cleaning service to lighten my load. This freed up time for us to spend together. I guess you could say that in our case, we were buying time.

I discovered the therapeutic benefits of structure many years ago when we were going through infertility. We hoped for a baby, month after month, year after year. Finally, after yet another round of cutting-edge medical treatments fell short, I was left with two choices. I could continue to obsess about the lack of a baby...and probably go crazy. Or I could find a way to have a meaningful life while I waited.

One day, David spoke some words that helped me turn a corner. More than 30 years later, I still remember his words. We were at the beach, and I was again bemoaning my situation. He looked at me and said quietly, "I know how badly you want a baby. I do too." And then he paused, and said, "You'll never be happy with a baby unless you're happy without one."

Two hours and a long walk on the beach later, I returned. David barely remembers saying those words, but I can tell you, they were life-giving. Somehow I released my grip and surrendered the dream of ever having a baby into God's hands. "Lord, You do what You want. I will trust You no matter what." I let go of my dream, but held on to my hope.

I felt strangely free and had a new fire for change. I took stock of where I was. What I had. What I lacked. Where I could grow. In short, I began to *clean house.* This was part practical and part spiritual. I worked at redoing the fixer-upper we had purchased. Clearing out the clutter in my home helped me de-clutter my soul as well. Paint, wallpaper, and yard work were doable. I couldn't control when we would have a baby, but I could control these.

I also took stock of my physical "house." My health had suffered from all the infertility drugs and treatments. Plus, I had always been a junk food addict. A Snickers bar seemed like a perfectly acceptable breakfast to me. Because I had a thin frame, I had gotten away with a destructive diet for years. I found a good naturopath and began to eat organic and healthy, which wasn't easy or even embraced by most people three decades ago. I also became more intentional about exercise.

I discovered that structure and order kept me mentally healthy and able to stay positive. Keeping a disciplined schedule was actually quite healing. There was some comfort in controlling what I could control. I dealt ruthlessly with worry, which, as we've discussed, can be the most exhausting emotion of all. I was diligent to purge fear, or in Bible language, I took my thoughts captive (2 Corinthians 10:5). Guess you could also say I binged on faith.

Over time, I began to see that simple, daily disciplines are also mysteriously connected to hope. Small habits can lead to large actions, which somehow keep dreams alive. And dreams have wider-reaching and even world-changing impact. In time, our three children were born, but the lessons in structure remained with us.

As you might imagine, these habits spilled over to help David and our entire family. Because of my years of infertility, we developed healthy eating and exercise habits that have strengthened us, fortified our home, and helped us stay strong through nearly 40 years of marriage, family, and ministry.

Without realizing it, all the while David and I were going through our fiery trial, we were also training ourselves to sustain ourselves. This takes us back to our earlier understanding of *ezer* as a warrior. Let's remind ourselves that there is a war, however subtle it may seem, waged by the evil one against every home. And the warrior-like strength needed to guard our home is given to us by God to fight this ongoing battle. Structure helps to keep us alert and "always ready." This is vital to the strength of our homes and marriages.

Our High Calling

I hope you see by now that a commitment to fortify your home is a holy work. Covering your husband and children in prayer goes hand-in-hand with creating an environment that works well for the needs of your family. God never wants you to separate the practical part from the spiritual life of a home. Both are sacred. Home contains your family. So your role as "keeper" or *ezer* is crucial. If you don't guard your home, who will? For no one loves your family like you do.

And no one on Earth knows your husband like you do. No one knows the special words or actions that best communicate honor to him. No one can keep watch as carefully as you're called to do. You see the small problems before they become big ones. You sense the call to pray, or to guard against danger, or work toward a solution.

As women, we all have other activities, responsibilities, and friendships that require our time and energy. But God didn't give anyone else the task of being our husband's *ezer*. And He didn't equip anyone else with the gifts and passion He's given to us to fulfill this high calling.

6

Lighten His Load

DAVID AND I WERE invited to speak at a marriage event and share about practical ways for couples to build strong marriages. We decided to each make a list of the top-ten marriage tips that have been most valuable to us over the years.

Now I have to confess that I love lists. Just tell me the top-ten superfoods or the five best parenting tips. Show me eight great restaurants or the three best vacation spots. A list always hooks me! When our daughter Bethany was newly married, she would often call me for advice and say, "Mom, I need some tips on cooking, health, marriage, etcetera. Just give me a list." Like her mother, she likes a list.

David and I each compiled our own list. To create a little drama, we decided we wouldn't compare lists until we were actually up on stage speaking to the large gathering. So I shared my #10 tip and David shared his, and so on. There was some obvious overlap. Things like praying together, staying healthy, and being wise with our finances were on both our lists.

The fun came at the end of our message when we revealed our #1 tip to each other and the audience. Turns out we both had come up with exactly the same answer. Our #1 most important tip for making our marriage strong was simply this: We take a day off together every week.

Maybe you're thinking, *Is that all?* It sounds so anticlimactic. I'll talk more about the powerful impact that simply taking a weekly day off has had on our marriage and family life. But for now, I'll tell you that we have continued this habit throughout our nearly four decades together. And if asked, I'd say it again. Taking a day off together each week is our best piece of practical advice for any young couple who wants to sustain a long and happy marriage.

Many marriages today are running on empty. Finding tangible ways to help our husbands guard against overload is a good place to get fierce with our *ezer* role. I've learned that simple actions, such as taking a day off together, honor David by allowing him to be refreshed so he can return to the fray strengthened.

Rest is one way to help our husbands (and all of us, for that matter) be their best. Today's world is busy, noisy, and draining. It's getting more so every day. We need to lighten up. It's time to enjoy our marriages, not just endure them.

LEARN HOW TO REST

Be honest with yourself: Just how tired are you? And how tired is your husband? Are you getting enough sleep? Do you ever take a vacation? We're a culture obsessed with rest, or the lack of it. We're also sleep-deprived and apparently, we don't even know it. Our children's school sent parents an article on sleep deprivation in today's teens and adults. Did you know that sleep deprivation makes us more prone to accidents, weight gain, diabetes, and even heart disease?[1] Researchers tell us that people now fantasize about sleep more than sex. It would seem that the average person today is very, very tired.

But it's hard to help my husband rest if I'm exhausted myself. With our busy schedules, David and I have to work really hard to guard against overload. I've had to ask myself how effective I am at finding rest for my own soul. I can't give away what I don't have.

Even the ways we rest don't really rest us. Sometimes we drift into addictive or numbing behaviors that deaden our senses rather than rest our souls. Too much social media, too much work, too much alcohol, even too much exercise. You may be working harder, running faster, climbing higher, growing richer, getting thinner, and accomplishing more, but who's watching out for your soul?

And who's watching out for your husband, your marriage, and your family? Don't you long to do more than just damage control to manage the swirl of life? We have to get to the root of the problem if we truly want to lighten our load and guard our marriage against exhaustion. I try to help David read his emotional and physical energy gauges, and he helps me read mine. I've noticed that most of our arguments spring up when we're both exhausted. Just like children, we get cranky when we miss our rest.

The legendary football coach Vince Lombardi is popularly credited with once saying, "Fatigue makes cowards of us all."[2] I believe this applies to marriage as well. When husbands and wives are exhausted and our faith becomes weak, we're left vulnerable to enemies from within and without.

When working with pastors who had fallen into extramarital affairs, well-known Willow Creek pastor and author Bill Hybels observed that most had exhausted themselves into immorality.[3] This kind of behavior is not just the domain of men. I've also known wives to abandon their husbands. Sadly, I watched a successful pastor's wife leave her husband and children for another man. She's the last person I could have imagined falling prey to this temptation. A mutual friend made this wise observation: "She must have been exhausted."

Don't you wish we had a warning system that would alert us when we begin to drift into patterns of living that are dangerous to our soul?

It's no wonder marriages today are crashing and burning. It's time we find ways to guard our families against overload.

Dr. James Dobson, founder of Focus on the Family, says the most dangerous but often overlooked threat to today's marriages is over-commitment.[4] As far back as 40 years ago, Dobson gave this warning to couples in *What Wives Wish Their Husbands Knew About Women*: "Husbands and wives should constantly guard against the scourge of overcommitment," he cautioned. "Even worthwhile and enjoyable activities become damaging when they consume the last ounce of energy or the remaining free moments in the day."[5]

Think about how much faster our pace of life is now than when Dobson wrote those words four decades ago. Even though we try to set good boundaries, life sometimes throws us the unexpected and we're forced to operate on overload. No one is at their best when exhausted. It's ironic but true: We must work hard to find rest. I'm reminded of Hebrews 4:11, which encourages us to "make every effort to enter that rest." And while this passage speaks primarily to the rest Jesus offers through our salvation—we can't be saved by our good works—I think the same truth applies to physical rest. It takes effort and intentionality on our part if we are serious about getting rest.

David and I are not unique. Most people feel stressed by today's fast pace. The demands on your marriage are different from the demands on ours, so you and your husband will need to creatively explore the best ways for you to replenish yourselves. Let's dare to go against the grain of our culture. It's time to lighten the load and refresh our marriages.

Take a Day Off Together

David and I started our "Day Off" habit early in our marriage. Three weeks after our wedding, we packed up our U-Haul and moved to Houston, Texas, where David was to complete his doctoral intern-ship in ministry at a large, downtown church. We became fast friends with another young couple on staff who were committed to taking a day off together each week. This one simple habit, they said, was their best marriage secret.

Obviously, Sunday wasn't much of a rest day for us with all the church responsibilities we had. So we decided our weekly day off would be Tuesday. We grew to love Day Off so much that it was worth it to guard it. I even made it through my entire master's degree program in counseling without ever taking a class on Tuesdays.

Our Day Off routine started out simple. We were careful not to use that day as catch-up time for all our unfinished work. No housework or yard work either. Sometimes we went out for coffee and took time to catch up on our week and pray for the needs on our hearts. We always felt closer to God and to each other on Day Off. Often, we'd go out for breakfast. For years, we went to the same IHOP across town. We got to be such good friends with our two favorite waitresses, Pat and Jerry, that when we had our first baby, they would often take care of her while we enjoyed our meal. When Jerry's husband died, she called David, the only "pastor" she knew.

No matter how hectic our week was, we knew we were only days or hours away from Day Off. We would have time to talk things through. This kept small problems from escalating into big ones. These days, whenever we're asked to teach on marriage, we always end up talking about the value of taking a weekly day off together.

After the children entered school, we picked Friday as Day Off. We'd enjoy the day together until the kids got home from school. Friday night became known as "Pizza Family Home Night." We'd order pizzas or make our own, and watch a movie together. Our entire family looked forward to Day Off each week. Our grown kids now tell us how much they enjoyed those days. I'd also like to think they learned the value of rest in the middle of their own very busy lives.

Honestly, I understand why it may be hard for you and your husband to find time to take a day off together. It's a hard habit to form later in your marriage. Plus, there's the matter of the overwhelming workload you may carry.

I have to admit I tend toward workaholism, so learning to take a day off each week was challenging for me. I found it required trusting God with my work just like I learned to trust Him with our money. But in much the same way that tithing our income can break the back of greed, taking a day off seemed to break the back of work addiction. Americans, I've heard it said, are the only people who "worship their work, work at their play, and play at their worship."

Encourage your husband to tell you what helps him slow down and rest. Maybe you can't take a whole day off. Why not start small? Maybe a date night or morning coffee time works best for you. And be on the lookout for other ways to find rest on a daily basis. David encourages me to have a quitting time each day when I stop work and do something fun or replenishing.

And don't underestimate the power of a good nap. A friend of mine is a connoisseur of the perfect nap. Shoes and socks must be off, she said. Get all the way under the sheets with a good book. Set your alarm for one hour. Start reading and let yourself fall asleep naturally. The alarm will awaken you. Voila! The perfect nap.

In saying all this, I simply want you to see that rest is a necessity, not a luxury. We are not machines meant to work seven days a week. Without rest, our mental and physical health can suffer. Without rest, even love grows cold.

Keep the Sabbath

If you're like me, you probably spend a lot of your waking hours caring for those you love, scrambling madly to finish the to-do list each day. But who is telling you to guard your soul and to tend to your spiritual life? It's worth saying again: You're a better helper, or *ezer*, for your husband when you are spiritually strong.

You might be surprised at how often the Bible talks about the overall care of your soul. God looks at rest as an important part of family life. He ordained a day of rest into His framework of laws known as the Ten Commandments. He said, "Remember the Sabbath day by keeping it holy" (Exodus 20:8). Let's recall our earlier study of Titus 2:5, in which we learned that to *keep* means "to guard." We need to guard our Sabbath rest.

The word for Sabbath, or *Shabbat,* simply means to stop or to cease. The Bible includes more instructions about how to keep the Sabbath than all the other nine commandments.[6] Rest is a command. It impacts our worship, our prayer life, and our family. It's a good way to guard our marriages.

In addition to the actual Sabbath day, there were opportunities for "Sabbath rest." Woven into the fabric of Hebrew community life were numerous days and weeks of festivals and celebrations that gave families a chance to step back from the usual pace of life. God instructed the people to spend time together in worship, fellowship, feasting, and fun—kind of like mini-vacations. The Sabbath and other rest days were considered *holy*, or "set apart." We get our word *holiday* from this concept of "holy day." Even newlyweds in the ancient Hebrew culture enjoyed special consideration. They were encouraged to enjoy their first year of marriage as a time to grow together, free from heavy workloads or military service.

Our friends from other countries express surprise at how little vacation time Americans take with their families. Formerly from South Africa, where "holidays," as they call them, are a priority, our friends Bryan and June have always treasured extended rest times with family. Bryan once noted that "Americans seem afraid of taking holidays, lest they get behind in their work." Even travel agents now receive frequent requests to plan short three- to four-day mini-excursions instead of longer family vacations.

I find this trend sad. David and I have noticed it takes the first few days of a vacation to simply unwind enough to enjoy the rest of it.

We guard family vacation time just like we guard our day off. Vacations are a priority, and we've tried to be creative with travel. We even started a vacation fund early in our marriage, saving a little money each month for family times away. We consider Day Off, Sabbath rest, and family vacations all to be secrets to sustainability.

The Power of Play

I remember a line from a popular children's movie from decades ago that went something like this: "Every kid knows that daddies mean fun and mommies mean business." It's a familiar scenario even today—dad is befuddled and mom jumps in to solve the problem and save the day.

I believe this message sells dads short. Because sometimes *fun* is exactly what we need to get through a crisis. David's playful sense of humor can sometimes defuse a tense situation faster than any amount of my reasoning. I've discovered that one way I can help keep our home peaceful is by responding to his lighthearted approach and refusing to take problems—or myself—quite so seriously.

It's also true that another way to help lighten our husband's load is to appreciate the unique power of playfulness. It didn't take long into our marriage for me to see that watching sports was one way David could unwind from the relentless demands of ministry. I should have had a clue when he watched all six basketball games of the NBA Finals on our honeymoon! Maybe a little extreme, he now admits.

But over the years, I actually came to appreciate sports as one more way to help our family unwind. I recently asked our daughter Bethany what she liked about our household growing up. She remembered how her dad was playful, helping us keep things light even when we faced minor crises in our family.

During our years of infertility when I continually faced invasive medical treatments, drugs, and surgeries, David knew how to help me persevere. His playfulness enabled me to keep a light heart through some of our darkest moments until we finally had our babies. It's true what they say: "He who laughs, lasts."

David's approach may be lighthearted at times, but he also knows how to calm anxiety in times of extreme crisis. One of his strengths is giving hope when all looks hopeless. Over the years, I've watched him walk people through countless life-and-death situations. He even helped counsel our community through the shocking aftermath of 9/11 as a guest radio commentator for the entire week following the attacks. "As long as the sun comes up in the morning," he would tell listeners, "there's always hope." These daily "Moments of Hope" became so popular that our city's largest secular radio station made them a daily feature and invited David to do a weekly Sunday morning faith and values program.

Playfulness is related to joy and can be a powerful weapon against major stress. Our friends Michael and Kathleen discovered this when they faced a life-threatening crisis. Ten years ago, Kathleen discovered she had lung cancer. After her fiercely brave fight and eventual recovery, Michael decided to sell his business. The two feisty grandparents decided to build a log cabin in the mountains. They also bought a couple of Harleys and began riding their motorcycles all over the country, visiting more than 40 states and countless National Parks together. They've learned the restorative power of fun.

Kids understand the value of play better than anyone. I had to laugh when our youngest son, Michael, who was about six at the time, pointed out to me with complete seriousness: "You know, Mom, a boy can't live without toys." Jesus must have understood the power of play. He especially loved children and once warned that if we didn't become like little children, we couldn't enter the kingdom of heaven.[7]

This concept became especially clear while I was enjoying a cup of tea one afternoon with my then-four-year-old granddaughter, Anna Grace. She was feeling quite grown up as she carefully balanced the delicate china cup and saucer on her lap. We were talking about all kinds of things when the conversation shifted gently to more spiritual matters. I sensed a teachable moment. "Guess what Jesus tells grown-ups?" I said to her. "He says we have to be like little kids if we want to know Him better. Why do you suppose Jesus likes kids so much?" She thought for a moment, then answered, "Because we're so fun to play with." Turned out the teachable moment was actually for *me*.

Play restores our soul. Laughter and fun help tone down the drama in our homes. Men often feel anxiety but may internalize it more than women. So encourage your husband to let you know what helps lighten his load. Respond to his humor. Create fun in your home. Laugh with your children. Laugh about mistakes. Laugh in good times and hard times. Have fun. And remember, play refreshes us. That's why we call it recreation.

Cultivate Contentment

Most husbands feel a burden to provide for their family whether or not they're the sole breadwinner. Work is woven into the heart of man and existed before the Fall. Hard work is honorable and fulfilling. It was given by God as a good gift.[8] But after the man and woman chose to rebel against God, everything in life suddenly became an uphill climb. "In pain you shall bring forth children," God said to the woman.[9] Even the ground became stubborn and cursed, so work would become a burden for the man. Growing food turned into an exhausting task, accomplished only through the "sweat of [his] brow."[10]

Let's fast-forward to today. Our desire for more possessions can cause us to work harder and rest less. This drive to acquire more puts yet another burden on already-stressed marriages. We've discussed how the fast pace of life drives us to overload. Added to that is the lie that we need more possessions to be happy. This means we must watch out for greed, another stealth invader that can easily rob our homes of peace. To do this requires vigilance on our part.

Guard Against Greed

When I was growing up in the Deep South, a common saying was, "If mama ain't happy, ain't nobody happy." Or here's another one: "Happy wife, happy life." There's some truth to the fact that, as women, our emotions impact those around us. To a degree, we set the emotional climate of our home. Especially when it comes to contentment.

I can lighten David's emotional load by being content with what we have. Thankful for what he provides. Over the years, I've tried to resist the pressure to have more and more. It's a constant battle, since we live in a world that bombards us with the message that enough is never enough. Guarding our home against greed is another way to be *ezer* strong.

Early in our marriage, it dawned on me that a practical way to keep a lid on greed was simply to limit the size of our home. I happened to mention this idea to a few friends as we wrestled with the issue of greed. If we didn't constantly build "bigger barns,"[11] I reasoned, then perhaps our possessions would have a natural boundary. This strategy would still allow us to enjoy beautiful furnishings and a tastefully decorated home.

David and I have now been comfortable and contented in the same home we've loved for nearly 30 years. I recently talked with one friend who had been part of that discussion years earlier about "bigger barns." She made it a point to tell me that our conversation had influenced decisions she and her husband made over the years. As their wealth grew, they had decided to limit the size of their home. She was thankful they had managed to keep a balanced perspective on possessions and guard against greed.

Social media now brings us face-to-face with even greater pressure to "keep up with the Joneses." Now the Joneses can create their own digital presence where image is everything. Consequently, life for the Joneses can look perfect, even if dysfunctions loom beneath the surface. How easy it is to buy into their deception and fall prey to the temptation to compare our insides with their outsides. Researchers have found that the number one emotion people experience when getting on Facebook is envy. It's easy to see how we can easily fall into what my husband calls "the snare to compare." This can lead to greed, which the Bible clearly calls idolatry.[12] It's also coveting, something God clearly forbids.[13]

Greed is not only exhausting, it's addictive—who hasn't heard of *shopaholics*? But it has an even more sinister side. There's the famous case of traitor Aldrich Ames, the counterintelligence agent for the CIA for 31 years who was convicted of spying against the United States. Ames sold the identities of our government's valuable double agents to the Russian KGB for millions of dollars, resulting in the execution of nearly a dozen CIA operatives. He turned against his country and caused massive loss of life, all for greed.

Apparently Ames's second wife was equally greedy and at least part of the motivation for his heinous betrayal of his country. She had in her possession more than 60 purses and 500 pairs of shoes in their lavish home when they were arrested in 1994. Ames is now serving a life sentence without the possibility of parole for his crimes.[14]

I want to point out an intriguing contrast between this example of greed and our earlier study of the Proverbs 31 wife. "The heart of her husband trusts in her," we are told, "and he will have no lack of gain" (Proverbs 31:11 esv). A closer look into the Hebrew text implies that her husband had no need of *dishonest* gain. The Wycliffe Bible translation from the late 1300s puts it this way: "The heart of her husband trusteth in her; and he shall not have need to robberies. (Her husband trusteth her in his heart; and he shall have no need for robbery, or for theft)" (Proverbs 31:11 wyc).[15] In other words, her husband wasn't forced to steal to support his wife's greed.

Chronic discontent can become a habit. It fuels overwork and ingratitude. And as I mentioned, it's a stealth invader in our marriages.

It even spills over to our kids, encouraging a sense of entitlement, not to mention the burden it can place on our husbands. When it comes to greed, nobody wins. It helps to have like-minded friends who can help us stay balanced and hold us accountable. Sometimes all it takes to break the hold greed has on us is to simply confess it to a friend.

Cultivating contentment is yet another way to trust God and grow strong in our relationship with Him. In so doing, we also honor our husband and lighten his load. Jesus promised in Matthew 6:33 that as we "seek first His kingdom," we'll find that all "these things"—the food, shelter, and clothing needs of life will be "given to you as well."

Keep Your Balance

It's easier to guard against greed when we keep a balanced life. But it's easy to drift to extremes where enough is never enough. We're never thin enough or rich enough or pretty enough. Instead of seeking balance, which is not as sexy as extreme, we drift to excess.

Simply having a nice home is not enough—we lust for more. One friend noticed her desires for "more and better" were fueled by the home decorating magazines she liked to read. She glibly referred to these magazines as "domestic porn." But she was genuinely bothered by how the pictures of perfectly decorated homes actually fueled her greed. So she decided to stop looking at the magazines altogether for a season and enjoy the things she had.

I like the way author Tim Keller explains it in *Counterfeit Gods*.[16] He says idolatry occurs when we make good things into ultimate things. We either won't wait for God to work, or we don't trust Him to meet our needs. Pretty soon, we find ourselves empty and exhausted by the very things we thought would make us free.

We've bought into the world's lies about what truly satisfies our soul. Idols may fill us up for a time, but the hope they provide is fleeting. Like Confederate money, their worth will one day be useless. Or as my husband says, "It's all gonna burn."

God calls us to balance. He wants us to enjoy material things, not be in bondage to them. He blesses us and "richly provides us with everything for our enjoyment."[17] Idolatry robs us of contentment and dishonors God. It's also exhausting, adding even more to our sense of overload.

The apostle John warned the early church, "Dear children, keep yourselves from idols" (1 John 5:21). In the Greek text, "keep" is the same word we saw in Titus 2 for "keeper" or "guard." We need to be fierce in guarding our home against the idolatry of greed. This is *ezer* at her best.

It's easy to find ourselves running in circles longing to be satisfied. As women, we're tempted to look to our image, comfort, or pocketbooks to fill our deepest longings. Pretty soon, we find ourselves empty and exhausted by the very things we thought would make us free. It's time to get ruthless with our idols. It starts with keeping our balance.

"Learn to Take a B"

I discovered a secret to keeping my balance. I call it "learning to take a B." Sometimes, giving my "B" effort is the best way to stay faithful to the big picture and avoid making good things into ultimate things, as Keller said. But I have to confess that taking a B goes against my grain. I'd much rather make A's. Growing up, I liked to compete in sports and schoolwork. I was a bit obsessive about making A's. Plus I liked setting tangible goals and reaching them.

After I graduated into the real world of work and eventually family, goals were harder to define. I discovered that some goals, such as being physically in shape, could actually work against more important priorities such as spending time with my husband or children, or serving God. This was especially true if I was intent on having an A workout body.

How could I achieve success in one area without completely sacrificing the other? I yearned for balance in my life. So I decided that "taking a B" in the area of fitness was plenty fit enough for me. That meant working out about thirty minutes a day, five times a week.

My routine was simple and sustainable. It was enough to keep me alert and in good health. It was not enough to give me perfectly sculpted abs, which I don't really need anyway. Especially when I compare that to the passion I have for a strong marriage or world-changing kids, or ministry—definitely worth my A effort.

Since then, I have noticed that learning to take a B in other areas has helped me sustain a more balanced life. For example, I like having a nice home and dressing well. But taking a B in those areas works just fine for now, and leaves me with the time, energy, and resources to focus on my A game.

My relationship with the Lord comes first. Then comes family. Being available as David's helper and raising our kids are top priorities. So is ministry, though even that took a back seat to our children when they were young.

Your priorities may be different, but I hope you get the point. Think about where you can take a B and become more balanced in your life. Your own activities and strategies for finding balance will be different from mine. Experiment with what works best for you. It's not about having less excellence, but rather, more balance. For me, B means balance, not mediocrity. It's sustainable. Best of all, balance helps me remain faithful over the long haul, and that honors God as well as my husband.

Give Your Life Away

Let's face it. When it comes to greed, it's a jungle out there. Envy can be toxic to marriages. As the keepers of our homes, we need to be continually on the lookout for ways to guard against greed and cultivate contentment.

David and I have learned that sharing what we have with others is another way to wage war in this ongoing battle against materialism. Something amazing happens when we serve others and share what we have with the poor. We will talk more about that in the next chapter.

One of my favorite Bible verses sheds light on this mystery. God promises that "if you spend yourselves in behalf of the hungry and satisfy the needs of the oppressed, then your light will rise in the darkness, and your night will become like the noonday."[18] In other words, when we give our life away, then our own darkness and gloom are lifted "like the noonday."

It's a mystery as to why, but giving lightens the heart. It's one of the most powerful ways to break the back of greed and materialism. It increases contentment and even joy. David and I have noticed that sharing with others helps us stay filled up and makes us less likely to go after false gods or idols.

Point Him to Jesus

It's important to find ways to lighten our husband's load. But in the end, our most valuable influence as his helper, or *ezer*, is to point him toward Jesus and the finished work of the cross. When we learn how to find our true rest and contentment in Christ, we're entering into what is known as "the rest of faith."[19]

Overwork and greed are modern-day idols. So it's wise to be aware that when we set our minds to guard against idolatry, we step into an intense spiritual battle. I believe materialism is the chief rival god of our age. That's why victory over the bondage to material things and pulling down the stronghold of busyness requires a fierce fight. It's also why, at its core, our real battle is to believe and takes place in prayer.

But let's remember: The Bible tells us the fight of faith is a "good fight." The victories we win are good ones. They're good for us, good for our husbands, and good for our families. Above all, when we are victorious in our spiritual battle against overload and greed, we honor God.

7

Dream Big Together

I STILL REMEMBER THE exact spot where I was standing in my kitchen that morning, more than 20 years ago, when I sensed God was asking me to do something that seemed very risky but also very right. I said *yes*, and my life was forever changed. Through this episode, I also learned that one of the most powerful ways I can honor David is to share his dreams.

Has God ever given you a dangerous assignment? If your answer is yes, that tells me two things about you. First, you know how to listen to the voice of God. And second, you have the courage to obey. In both the Old and New Testaments, the words translated "hear" and "obey" are pretty much the same. Implicit in hearing God's voice is that you do what He asks you to do.

David and I happened to be giving a birthday breakfast that morning for our daughter Bethany. She was turning seven. To celebrate, we had prepared a feast of waffles and omelets and welcomed about a dozen noisy, lively first graders into our kitchen.

I was preoccupied as I prepared the meal. David had just accepted an invitation from a missions organization called Serving in Mission (SIM[1]) to go to Ethiopia—it would be his first time traveling to that part of the world. The invitation came on the heels of Ethiopia's long and brutal civil war. David had been asked to speak at a conference for thousands of believers there. The oppressive Communist regime had recently been overthrown. Christians were finally free to worship in public after nearly two decades of extreme persecution.

But Ethiopia was not yet stable or even considered safe for international travelers. I had been wrestling through an intense spiritual struggle for several weeks and had finally come to terms with letting David go. The journey would take him to Ethiopia's remote interior for nearly three weeks, during which time we would have little to no communication. This was before short-term missions travel to Africa was common. David and I like to say we developed a heart for Africa before Africa was "cool."

News reports coming out of Ethiopia were still not good. There were isolated incidents of violence, and the State Department alerts advised caution. But our friends at SIM believed the opportunity outweighed the risk.

The last time Christians had gathered at the Wolaita Conference, where David would be speaking, many had been arrested, tortured, and imprisoned in what would be one of the most brutal anti-Christian regimes in African history. We were sobered by the price these courageous Ethiopian believers had paid for their faith.

It was a conversation with a friend from church that first sparked my idea of going with David. JoAnn and her husband, Howard, had served as missionaries in Africa for years. Howard, who was the son of missionaries, had also grown up in Ethiopia. Howard and JoAnn Brant were now leaders with SIM.

"David's life is going to be dramatically changed by this trip," JoAnn said. "So will his vision for Forest Hill." She paused, then looked at me and said, "I don't know if you could possibly go. But it would be so powerful for you to experience this with David so you can share his dreams for Africa and be part of what God will do in this church." I couldn't shake her words.

But our children seemed so young—barely seven and three. How could I possibly leave them? "God," I prayed, "if You are calling me to go with David to Africa, You will have to be *really* clear. Someone will have to offer to keep our children—without my asking." An unlikely prayer, since few knew about the trip.

The following Sunday, a dear friend who had two children about the same ages as ours, came up to me and said, "I don't know if you've considered going with David. But, if you do, I'd like to keep Bethany and DB." Later, my dad called out of the blue and said, "If you're thinking about going with David, your mother and I would like to help with the children." So we had not one, but two sets of sitters to care for our children.

I was still a little anxious. I'd never left the children for more than a couple of nights at a time. This trip would take us to the other side of the Atlantic Ocean. The thought of an entire ocean separating me from my young children almost made me nauseous. I felt a little like Gideon as I asked God for further confirmation.

Soon after, during my morning quiet time, my eyes fell upon these verses: "If I rise on the wings of the dawn, if I settle on the far side of the sea, even there your hand will guide me, your right hand will hold me fast" (Psalm 139:9-10). Peace filled my heart as I reflected on the words. For me to fly to "the far side of the sea" and be an ocean away from my children could not separate me from the hand of God or from the "right hand" of His protection.

Later, while heading to my car, I happened to notice a small bookmark (the kind with a tassel at the top) lying face-down on my garage floor. *Where did this come from?* I wondered. I picked it up and stood transfixed as I read the verses, the *exact* words which I had been pondering. "If I rise on the wings of the dawn, if I settle on the far side of the sea, even there your hand will guide me, your right hand will hold me fast."

And so, while cooking waffles and omelets that morning, I sensed

God's whisper. He was gently chiding me as one would a dearly loved child: "You don't have to go to Ethiopia. David is certainly not putting any pressure on you. You are free to follow your own desires for a safe life. Or you can choose to let go and entrust the children to Me. You have a chance to share David's dreams. And if you do, I can promise you'll have an incredible adventure."

I looked into the face of our daughter as she happily enjoyed her birthday party and peered into the eyes of our barely three-year-old son, and I said *yes* to God. A short time later, I would find myself looking into the faces of thousands of Ethiopian believers lined up in tight rows, seated on the hillside at the Wolaita Conference. David preached to what was estimated to be more than 25,000 gathered that day. Many had walked for miles to hear a message from God's Word. They listened in rapt attention with characteristic Ethiopian stillness, interrupted only by the occasional high-pitched "joy yell." I was overwhelmed by the vibrant joy of a people who had suffered so much for their faith.

We then traveled by helicopter to an even more remote region and experienced what I can only describe as the most exuberant foot-washing service imaginable. David and I got our feet washed—complete with a ceremony of great praise, worship and dancing, and Ethiopian joy yells—all the way up past our knees!

Next to getting married and giving birth to our three children, this journey to Ethiopia ranks as one of the most magical blessings in my life. It not only opened the door for us to eventually travel to 11 African countries, it paved the way for our church's involvement in Africa. Countless members have become heavily involved in missions work, and several have made bold decisions to live in Africa as missionaries. We've seen God mightily at work as the gospel continues to spread. Plus, we now have lifelong brothers and sisters in the faith all over the continent.

As for me, I discovered that when David and I dream big *together*, we're likely to embark on unexpected and life-changing adventures.

Why Dream Big?

There's hardly a better feeling on Earth than the one you get when a dream comes true. Think of the brave hero who fights for a noble dream. The greater the opposition, the more majestic the story. Victory brings honor to the dreamer. It's the stuff of which all great epic tales are made.

One of the things I love about David is that he dares to dream big dreams. So naturally, one of the best ways I can honor him is to support his dreams. Think for a minute. What are some of your husband's dreams? What are yours?

David and I have discovered that our dreams can motivate us and guide us toward God's purposes for our lives. Dreams make us stronger in our faith. And dreams are somehow connected to our destiny.

Dreams Connect Us to Our Calling

Looking back, David and I see that God was leading us along the path of our dreams even as children. I've wondered if God places specific dreams in our heart at an early age to draw us to His calling. Mother Teresa rightly said that we should tread gently around the dreams of children, for we "may be treading on the dreams of God." David and I believe God was drawing us to Himself through our dreams. And though we didn't know it at the time, He was also drawing us to each other.

David's childhood dreams included basketball. He describes himself as a shy, awkward middle school kid until a coach discovered he could play basketball. Basketball eventually led him to play for Coach Dean Smith at the University of North Carolina and later in the European Professional Leagues in Belgium and France.

According to David, basketball took him to places he never dreamed possible, such as traveling with a Christian basketball team who smuggled Bibles behind the Iron Curtain into what was then Communist Yugoslavia. He also played before thousands when UNC won the NIT Championship in Madison Square Garden. These kinds of experiences helped prepare the formerly shy young man to speak before thousands on a weekly basis.

Only after David came back to the United States to study for a counseling degree and served as a graduate assistant basketball coach at University of Florida did he stop resisting what had been God's persistent call to the ministry. As he tells the story, it was on a summer day in 1976, in a quiet apartment in Gainesville, that he responded to what he knew to be God's voice. As he puts it, "I finally quit running from the ministry."

As for me, I was also running—from God. At around 15, I had invited Him out of my life, though I had grown up going to church with loving Christian parents. I was determined to find my own path in life—without God.

Like David, I had big dreams. I studied journalism and international communication in college and wanted to be a world-changer. I was also deeply troubled by racism. My family had moved to Georgia when I was eight. I still remember the afternoon I walked through our small town for the first time. Curious about the brass sign hanging over a doorway, I asked, "Daddy, what does KKK mean?" I caught my breath as he explained the realities of racism in the South in the 1960s.

Ten years later, as our high school's cheerleading captain, I would face the privilege and challenge of welcoming the first African-American cheerleader in our school's history.

I continued to resist God. But all the while I thought I was running from God, He was quietly pursuing me. Sensing I was searching for truth, a Christian friend put a book into my hands one day and urged me to read it. It sat on my shelf for a year. But when I finally opened the dusty copy of *Mere Christianity* by C.S. Lewis, I was compelled to put my entire life and all my dreams into God's hands.

My first prayer was to ask God for a Christian husband. "Lord, please help me find a man who loves You with his whole heart." Then I remember thinking, *Lord, it would be great if he could be an athlete. Oh, and with a sense of humor. And would You mind making him tall...and if it's not too hard, I would like for him to be musical.* A lot to ask for someone who had been running from God.

A short time later, friends set us up on a blind date. I opened the door to this 6'7" former basketball player with a love for God and a good sense of humor. Turns out David even had a nice touch with the guitar. I began to see that perhaps God's plans for my life were to be far better than my own.

David and I were married less than a year later. The company I worked for granted me a leave to go to Houston for 15 months, where David would complete his doctoral internship. My job would be waiting when we returned. But after catching the excitement of sharing in the ministry with David, I chose not go back to the corporate world with its high ambitions and large salary. Such dreams no longer seemed big enough.

And when a small church in Charlotte called David to be their senior pastor, we sensed God's plan was unfolding. The church and its neighborhood were declining and we were advised not to go. But we fell in love with the people, their big dreams, and their giant heart for God. A small group had been meeting weekly, praying fervently for God to send them a man who would unashamedly preach the gospel. We never interviewed anywhere else.

Together, we sensed God's call to Forest Hill Church and dreamed of having an impact on our city and even the world with this amazing group of fellow dreamers. And we have never left. What began as 150 members has grown to 6000 on 5 campuses throughout the city. Our missions impact spans several continents. Our dreams connected us to each other and brought us to the calling where we have stayed for more than 35 years.

Dreams Build Our Faith

"Men grow great by their dreams," said Woodrow Wilson. I wonder if the opposite is true. Do men fail to achieve greatness when they stop dreaming? Most dreams aren't fulfilled without a fight. I find I'm fiercest in my *ezer* role when defending David's dreams—especially through prayer.

The more fervently David dreams to reach the world with the gospel, the more opposition he encounters. That's why big dreams call for courage and endurance. Hard work. Seeking God daily in prayer. Every God-given dream, at some point, will require a fight of faith. I guess you could say we are trained by our trials as we pursue our dreams. Or as one minister put it, we're being strengthened by those very hardships so that when our dreams finally come true, we are not crushed by the weight of their glory.

I have already mentioned the importance of prayer for our husbands. Sharing their dreams is like the other wing of the airplane. Not only are dreams and prayers compatible, but big dreams energize bold prayers. I don't believe our God-given dreams can become realities without prayer. And our faith grows as we step out in faith and say yes to God again and again.

I recently read an editorial by a young millennial writer who believes dreams are an unnecessary burden placed on her generation. She said big dreams only give false hope and raise unrealistic expectations that are bound to end up in disappointment. I disagree. I believe dreams, even lofty ones, give us a reason to get up in the morning and propel us toward something bigger than ourselves. Big dreams give us energy when we grow faint. We grow stronger in our gifts and talents as we pursue our dreams.

I realize it's cool these days to be cynical. "Don't dare to try too hard," is the subtle message. "And don't rise above your peers." While visiting their country several years ago, I learned that New Zealanders call this "the tall poppy syndrome." This thinking greatly concerns parents. Sports teams even have a hard time convincing players to give their best, lest they rise up above their peers. "Tall poppies," confided the mother of one fine New Zealand basketball player, "are often cut down when they succeed." No matter where you live, it takes courage and faith to dream big in today's world.

A dream is a mighty thing. Enemy forces are always waiting to crush dreams. David and I have prayed for God to guard our children's dreams. We've prayed He will use those dreams to draw them close to Him. To open doors for them to make an impact for Christ on this broken and hurting world. If a dream is truly given by God, we can be sure He is quietly at work behind the scenes to strengthen and sustain us.

Dreams build faith and help us endure when the work gets hard. "Miss Pat" ministered for decades to the children in one of the poorest slums in Savannah, Georgia. She said this to me when I asked how she persevered through the challenges of her sometimes grinding work in the city: "It was my calling that brought me here, and my calling keeps me here."

I took a risk years ago to obey God and honor David by sharing his dream for Africa. As it turned out, that decision made my own faith stronger. I discovered that my fear left and my courage grew. As for answering the call to the small church with big dreams? That opened the door to more impact than I could have imagined. My earlier dreams to be part of world change and racial reconciliation also came true as I worked with at-risk students in the urban community here in Charlotte and among genocide survivors in Africa.

Our hard-fought battles along the way only helped us to grow our faith as we built a legacy of watching God work. I would agree with David: If you're going to dream at all, dream big. Dream dreams so big only God can accomplish them.

Miracles Still Happen

I had no idea the simple silver key chain was such a source of encouragement for David. That is, until I found it in his drawer the other day. Thirty years have passed since I gave him the sterling disc with these three words inscribed on it: *Miracles Still Happen*.

I had given it to him as a reminder of how God had performed a miracle when I was healed from infertility. After four years of medical treatments and surgeries, waiting and praying, we finally had baby Bethany.

Now we needed a different kind of miracle. We had been at our church for about 6 years at the time, and our congregation had grown from about 150 to 500 members, outgrowing its small facility on Woodlawn Road. Our leaders were considering a piece of property that was being sold by another organization in town. The asking price back in 1986 was huge at $5 million, but it would give us 25 acres of prime land complete with several buildings.

The property and its buildings seemed perfect, but purchasing it was more than a long shot. It looked impossible. We were not a wealthy church. We needed a miracle. David is a big dreamer, but even for him, this was a giant leap of faith. But the leaders continued to pray. They sought wise counsel and explored the various financial options.

Sometimes on our days off, David and I would load up our tiny baby Bethany in the back of our VW Rabbit and drive around the property. We would pray and dream and ask God for another miracle. We wondered if He would do it again.

Over the next few months, too many miracles occurred and too many people stepped up to the plate for me to be able to tell the whole story here. But our humble, faith-filled congregation managed to raise the money and purchase the property.

Later, when we needed to build a sanctuary on the property to accommodate our growth, David and the elders sensed God was asking our church to first build a sanctuary for Community Outreach, an inner-city church with whom we had a close relationship. And so began our "Brick by Brick" campaign. Another miracle of provision occurred as God's people gave sacrificially. David and I, as well as many others, decided to double tithe, putting us in what we called the "gulp gift" range. In time, after completing Community Outreach Church, we had another campaign to raise funds for our own sanctuary.

Forest Hill Church, which started as the small church with big dreams, now has 5 campuses. The property we purchased has become our central campus, and our 6000 members have extended our church's witness throughout our community and to many parts of the world.

Back in the mid-1980s, that first leap of faith felt enormous. David says the silver key chain reminds him of that big, God-sized dream. And of my support when he wondered if we could fulfill that dream.

What is your husband's big dream? Is there something

tangible you can do to remind him to keep believing? He may need you more than you know. And your small gesture, and especially your prayers, may give him the strength he needs to persevere.

WHY DREAM TOGETHER?

The psychologist rubbed his beard and peered at David over the top of his glasses. He seemed to be carefully scrutinizing my husband. "Mr. Chadwick, judging from your results on our tests, I want to encourage you to consider another line of work." Then he added, "There is nothing in these scores to indicate that you can withstand the intellectual and emotional rigors of the ministry."

David sat stunned. He had just taken a battery of standardized psychological tests as part of his seminary education. The tests were designed to screen out unlikely applicants to the ministry. The psychologist had almost sounded as if he rather enjoyed giving David the discouraging news.

I never met the man, but I dubbed him "the Dream Killer." For his intention that day was to talk my husband out of entering the gospel ministry. Never mind that David had already earned master's and specialists' degrees in counseling. Or that he had made excellent grades in grad school. He was going by "the book." David asked the psychologist what he was supposed to do with his sense of being "called by God into the ministry." The guy just hemmed and hawed and said he didn't put much stock in such things.

All these years later, I can still remember how deflated David was after that encounter. But thankfully, he was confident he had heard God's clear call on his life. Upon prayer and reflection, we both sensed that this was a time of testing. We were to hold fast to God's calling. I remember feeling an overwhelming *ezer*-like desire to help David stand strong and resist the temptation to succumb to discouragement.

After nearly four decades of ministry under his belt, the comment I hear most frequently from people is the respect they have for David's ability to prepare powerful sermons week after week. The workload of preaching three times each weekend, combined with radio, speaking engagements, and writing books, would challenge men half his age. Plus, I cannot remember a single time in the last 35-plus years that David has been anxious or unprepared to preach. He loves his work. I guess you could say that no standardized test can measure a sense of God's call.

We Grow Close

David and I have learned that when we dream together, we grow closer to each other. We are marriage partners and best friends. But we're also teammates. Our shared dreams, and especially the tests and trials that go along with those dreams, knit us together like comrades in war. Even the discouraging report from the psychologist only forged a stronger bond, making us like a "band of brothers."

This was especially true when we were raising our children. We were both passionate about the shared dream of launching our kids to glorify God. It's no wonder God designed marriage and the family as the best vehicle for propagating the human race.

Let's go back to Genesis 2:18, our key verse on marriage in the Bible. The Lord God said, "It is not good for the man to be alone. I will make a helper suitable for him." It was God Himself who said it was "not good" for humans to be alone.

To solve the problem of aloneness for Adam, God didn't create a club, or a classroom, a corporation, social media, a team, or an army. He made a "helper," *ezer*, a corresponding but equal companion and a rock of support. He also created a lifelong covenant relationship called "marriage" between a man and a woman. Male and female. One flesh. Until death. Together, a couple would be capable of creating more humans and nurturing them to adulthood. A chore made easier because they would discover a sacrificial love for each other that was fiercer than the love they felt for themselves.

Perhaps you're thinking about your own family right now. Or the family you hope to have one day. You and your husband have been uniquely gifted for the family God has given you. The Bible says you are "God's handiwork, created in Christ Jesus to do good works, which God prepared in advance for us to do" (Ephesians 2:10). There is nothing like creating a home and family together to inspire big dreams. The point is to find ways you can dream big together.

Let's renew our zeal to guard our husbands and our marriages. What would happen if we were to become more intentional in sharing our husband's dreams? Because as much as I believe that individual success is rewarding, seeing a shared dream come true, in my experience, is sublime. Whoever said this was right: "The best way to achieve your own dreams is to help someone else reach theirs."

It's been an adventure to seek God's will with David on dreams ranging from our initial call to Forest Hill to the many global missions opportunities that have come our way. We had to hold fast to our dreams as we fought through exhausting years of infertility together. Then the birth and rearing of our three children and helping them pursue their dreams required its own special commitment. Just the other day we were reflecting on some of the incredible joys, heartaches, and challenges we had gone through together. We sat amazed at it all, especially grateful to be able to reflect on the journey—together.

The radical nature of a true conversion to Christ is never lost on me. I know full well what it means to go from darkness into light. When I gave my life to Christ, I didn't demand any promises of reward. I knew I was dying to myself, and in some ways it felt like death. But the beautiful irony is that whatever I gave up, I got back and more. Years later, I continue to marvel at how abundantly better it has been to follow God's plan for my life. His dreams for me were even better than my own. And what a privilege it has been to share my dreams with David—God's best gift of all.

We Get Strong

Marriage makes us stronger. And dreaming together brings its own special brand of strength to our marriage. We live in a world that constantly whispers in our ear, "It's all about you." Life is all about reaching *your* dreams. Your goals. Your best self. Narcissism has become the god of this age.

But the gospel throws us a curve with this message: It's all about putting *others* first. Honor each other above yourselves.[2] Husbands, love your wives. Wives, respect your husbands. Submit to one another in the Lord.[3] God's Word is radical when it comes to honor. We're even challenged to lay down our very lives for each other—an instruction to all believers, not just husbands and wives. We die to our rights and put another's honor before our own.

But the crazy thing is this: As I was trying to support David and adapt to his leadership and sharing his dreams, he was busy putting me first. We were practicing "honor each other above yourselves" without knowing it.

So whenever I worked to help David accomplish his dreams, my dreams were also fulfilled. Not too long into our marriage, I realized that God's economy is different from mine. When doing things God's way, I often get back the very things I give away. I help David reach his goals and dreams. Then he helps me reach mine. A wonderful rhythm develops. A mutuality.

Together, we've also learned that when we give our lives away, especially to the lost and broken of this world, God pours grace and honor back into our own lives. As I've shared in the case of my decision to go to Africa, sometimes our husbands' dreams may take us places that initially, we don't want to go. But as I trusted God, mysteriously, David's dreams actually became my dreams. And some of mine became his.

Relationships, and especially marriage, are God's best laboratory for growing our character. Making us stronger. Less selfish. As we live and work together, pray for each other, build each other up, and share each other's dreams, we actually become stronger people. And even when we bump, as couples often do, we are "iron sharpening iron."[4] Dreaming big together is one way God makes us stronger people, if we'll let Him.

We Last Long

An important part of marriage is learning to endure the inevitable ups and downs in life. We've seen how shared dreams are another way we become strong and form a bond that's not easily broken. No wonder the devil has his heart set on destroying dreams and dividing churches and families.

The Bible has this to say about the importance of unity:

> Two are better than one, because they have a good return for their labor: If either of them falls down, one can help the other up. But pity anyone who falls and has no one to help them up. Also, if two lie down together, they will keep warm. But how can one keep warm alone? Though one may be overpowered, two can defend themselves. A cord of three strands is not quickly broken (Ecclesiastes 4:9-12).

The principle in this passage is applicable to the church. When believers operate together in love and unity, they are better able to stand their ground against the opposition of the enemy. But the passage applies to marriage as well. When we stand together, we can fight off the opposing forces around us and guard our marriages and families.

This same truth is captured in the ancient Aesop's fable about the old man who was concerned about the constant quarreling among his grown sons. He gathered them together and handed each son a bundle of sticks to break. When fastened together, the bundle could not be broken. But when the old man took each stick out separately, they were easily snapped. He was teaching his sons that their unity was their greatest strength when up against an enemy. He warned them to guard their unity at all costs.

It's time to take seriously the need to guard the unity of our marriages and the church so we may stand strong against our enemies from within and without. I hope you're getting a clear picture of how our dreams play an important role in building and protecting our families. Dreaming big together helps us to go the distance in marriage.

Our Dreams Matter

The bottom line is this: Our dreams matter to God. Dreams can connect us to our life's calling and motivate us to grow in our faith. And when we dare to dream together with our husbands, we strengthen our marriage bond. Shared dreams not only help us grow closer and get stronger in our marriage, they also help us sustain our lifelong commitment to each other.

It's all about honoring our covenant no matter what happens. This example impacts our kids, our community, the church, and the watching world. For what good are big dreams if we don't finish strong?

8

Create a Culture of Honor

DAVID AND I SQUEEZED the last of our belongings into the U-Haul, said good-bye to my family in Atlanta, and started the long drive to Houston, Texas. We'd been married for only three weeks and had recently returned from our honeymoon. David had accepted an internship at a large church in Houston as part of his Doctorate in Ministry program.

It was still a little hard to believe I had gone from being an agnostic to a pastor's wife in such a short time. Just two years earlier while finishing college, I was being recruited for my dream job in Atlanta. But my life had taken a dramatic turn after placing my faith in Christ. Soon after that, I met David on a blind date, and we were married nine months later. It had been a whirlwind of change!

But I was deeply in love with David and passionate to follow the Lord wherever that took me. The fifteen-month internship would not only give us practical ministry experience, it would also give us a chance to adjust to married life. We didn't know a soul in Houston. Plus, I had taken a leave from my job of less than a year, cutting our income by well over half. It was a big move.

At the time, I didn't know much about the Bible and even less about being a wife. Imagine my surprise when we learned that our assignment was to start a class on marriage for recently married couples. What was the church's pastor thinking? I was pretty sure everybody on our class list had been married more than three weeks!

But many young people had drifted away from the church. The senior pastor, whom everyone affectionately called "Dr. Jack," must have figured that a former basketball player like David and ex-sorority girl like me might just be able to bring young couples back into the church. He wisely enlisted the help of a wonderful woman named Martha. She and her husband, Jim, had been longtime leaders in the church and had four grown kids. Martha had a heart for young couples, lots of great ideas, and boundless enthusiasm. The three of us decided to call our group the Carpenter's Class. Our hope and prayer was that together we could learn to build strong Christian marriages.

Armed only with our dreams and a sincere belief in God's Word, we sent a letter to everyone on the long list of young couples and invited them to the first class. Recently, while going through some old papers, I came across a copy of that letter. It was dated July 1978:

> Dear Friends,
>
> Did you know that in this country almost one out of two marriages are ending in divorce? Experts say that 40% of the children born today will live in a single parent home at some point in their lives. Frightening? You bet. But consider this statistic: In families where Bible reading and prayer are daily ingredients, divorce occurs in only one out of about 800 marriages. In light of these statistics, a group of recently married couples in the church has expressed an interest in forming a class to explore ways to help build strong Christian marriages. We will take a look at what the Bible teaches us about God's plan for marriage. We look forward to forming a strong fellowship in Christ among recently married couples. Not

only can we support each other, but together we can begin to make marriage what God intends it to be.

In His Service,

David, Marilynn, and Martha

The first Sunday, our room was full, and soon we had to move to a larger classroom. We grew rapidly to include around 60 couples. David taught a simple lesson from the Bible each week. It turned out that many of these young couples didn't know any more about the Bible than I did. We learned. We prayed. And we did life together.

David started a small group for some of the guys who wanted to go deeper. I began one for the wives—my first attempt ever at leading a Bible study. Some of the wives were on their own spiritual search and full of questions. It helped that I could speak their language.

I was barely a step ahead of them as we explored what the Bible had to say about marriage. These young wives were cute and fun. They were also ready to take God at His Word—eager to build strong marriages. "Girls, it says here in the book of Ephesians that we're supposed to honor and respect our husbands as the spiritual leaders of our homes." "Okay, since this is God's Word," they'd reply, "let's do it." And we did.

Our faith at that point was almost childlike. We were beginners. But if prayer and Bible study would help us build solid marriages, we were all in. We also learned how vital it was to surround ourselves with like-minded teammates. We were truly a team of *ezers*.

Our journey together became kind of a marriage laboratory. David and I learned right along with our new friends and tried to practice what we taught. We didn't do everything perfectly. But God's grace helped us, and Martha was our rock. I'd like to think the other couples grew as much as we did. They proved to be enthusiastic learners and became the dearest of friends. The class included young couples from all walks of life—investment bankers, construction workers, lawyers, a doctor or two, some government workers, and several in the oil business. Many went on to become strong leaders in the church and raise wonderful families.

Our fifteen months with the Carpenter's Class helped lay the foundation for the next four decades of our marriage and ministry. We formed simple habits and practiced them over time. I would discover how valuable these early lessons were when, later on, we had our three children.

All through this book, we've been talking about ways to honor our husbands. Recently I asked David how our family life together had honored him. He thought for a minute, then said, "The children have honored me most by believing what I believe. That's the greatest honor in my entire life."

The home can be a wonderful laboratory in which to cultivate honor. The tone we set in our homes when we honor our husbands can inspire our children to honor him and each other. It feels good to get respect. To be honored. But it feels even better to honor someone else. We find that as we give honor away, we get it back.

In many ways, showing honor is so simple a child can grasp it—but somehow it's disappearing from our homes and our culture. If we agree that honor is such a good thing, I wonder why we're missing the mark.

WHY ARE WE SO THIRSTY?

The reality show star was being interviewed about her upcoming plastic surgery—simply one more in her quest for the perfect face and body. She was now in her second celebrity marriage and the mother of half a dozen kids. Cameras took viewers up close and personal to witness her surgery. Then, they went behind the scenes to peek into the private world of her family. This was her reality—or at least her reality TV show.

I felt a bit sad for the woman and found myself wondering—was all this really worth the price? She'd lost her privacy. And her self-respect. The toll on her physical and emotional health must have been staggering. One marriage had gone down the tubes. Where would this one be in five years? I thought about her kids—a collection from two marriages and counting. What kind of legacy was she leaving them? Surely this was about more than just money. Maybe the payoff she was seeking could be summed up in one word: *fame*.

Fame can be defined as the condition of being "known or recognized by many people."[1] But fame is fleeting. It comes with no guarantees of permanence. Honor, on the other hand, is solid. Weighty. Lasting. Honor brings respect and esteem.

The desire to be known is not in itself a bad thing. In fact, the longing to be truly known is woven into our very being, put there by God. Let's remember it was God Himself who said it's "not good for the man to be alone" (Genesis 2:18). But being famous, or widely known, is not the same as being deeply known. We're thirsty for honor. But all too frequently we're willing to sell our souls for the cheap wine of fame.

It's no wonder we're so thirsty for honor as we watch the culture around us become more and more saturated with dishonor and disrespect. When honor is gone, so is our shield against danger and shame. Deep inside, we're all more vulnerable when honor is lacking, and we know it.

Ultimately of course, our thirst is for God. Only through a relationship with Jesus can we find the forgiveness that frees us from shame, protects us from danger, releases us from the need to be addicted to fame and other idols. But like my good friend Janet says, "Sometimes you have to wipe the mud out of someone's eyes before they can see Jesus." Perhaps creating a culture of honor is a good place to begin.

HONOR BEGINS AT HOME

When our kids were young, David and I used to tell them, half teasingly, that they had it easy when it came to obeying God. If they would just keep the fifth commandment, all the others would most likely fall into place.

There was actually some wisdom in what we said. The fifth commandment, addressed to children, was the first with a promise. God's Word teaches children that if they will honor their parents, they'll experience blessings: "Honor your father and mother"—which is the first commandment with a promise—"so that it may go well with you and that you may enjoy long life on the earth" (Ephesians 6:1-3).

"If your dad and I are not doing our job right," I'd say to them, "God will deal with us. So pray for us to hear God. He may even change our minds if we're wrong." Changing our minds to reconsider a decision in their favor was something that happened on more than one occasion, and it helped the kids to see that David and I were serious about listening to God.

Just imagine how many problems would be solved if children of all ages honored their parents. It's good for parents to receive honor. But it's even better for kids to give it. They grow best when they learn to honor and respect those in authority. Who knows the pain, problems, and failures kids could be spared if they learned to show honor?

Honoring parents is like the training wheels that help kids learn to honor God. God, in His wisdom, knows kids need to practice showing honor every day to their parents. He knows children thrive in a climate of respect. Then as our kids grow older, this honor toward parents can more easily transition to honor toward God.

I'll say it again: Home is the ideal laboratory for creating a culture of honor where the family can flourish. Maybe it's easier to think of culture as more like a *climate*. A climate affects everyone living under its influence, whether they're conscious of it or not. When a climate or an environment is healthy, everyone has a chance to grow and develop.

Right now you may be saying to yourself, *I thought this was a book about how to honor my husband.* It is, but let's remember that cultivating a home where honor is present and faith can flourish is a key way to respect your husband. This really hit home for me when David said that our kids' choice to walk with the Lord was the greatest honor in his life.

The kind of culture we create in our homes naturally spills over to the culture around us. But it takes time and intentionality, because when we create a culture of honor, we're going against the grain of the surrounding culture. That's why we need God's help. It takes faith, hard work, and lots of grace.

Keep the Faith

If there were one activity you could carry out that would dramatically increase the odds that your marriage would last, would you do it? Studies show that prayer can dramatically increase your chances of success. In a widely quoted 1980s study, Gallup researched how personal faith impacted marital satisfaction. They reported that when couples prayed together regularly, less than 1 percent of the marriages ended in divorce. Pretty amazing when the divorce rate in the general population is around 50 percent.[2] But here's some not-so-good news: About 92 percent of couples professing to be Christians don't pray together.

Now I don't think prayer is magic. But I do believe that when you pray and read the Bible together as a couple, you're inviting Christ's presence into your marriage. The Bible teaches that "a cord of three strands is not quickly broken" (Ecclesiastes 4:12). In our case, I like to think of those three strands as the Lord, David, and me. We've invited the presence of Jesus into our marriage and our home. And that changes everything.

Perhaps you and your husband don't pray together as a couple. You could be feeling a little discouraged right now, wondering if your husband would even want to pray, much less lead family prayer. Maybe he doesn't even believe in the Lord.

I want to encourage you to hold on to your hope. Over the years, I've seen God transform a husband's faith through the prayers of his wife time and again. Let's revisit the first chapter of this book, "First, Become Strong," and remind ourselves of the importance of our own relationship with the Lord.

Let's also remember the encouragement given to wives in 1 Peter 3:1, which tells us that even husbands who "do not believe the word" can be "won over without words" by the respectful behavior of their wives, which I imagine is also backed up by lots of prayer.

I've observed that one way a husband becomes inspired to pray with his wife is when he sees God answering her prayers—especially prayers for specific needs in their family. My prayer partner, Beth, and her husband, Gene, pray together regularly. He often shares his prayer requests with her. Even their five grown sons (and daughters-in-law) call Beth with PODs (short for "Prayers on Demand"). Beth is faithful to pray specifically and often, and they know it. They've all felt the presence and power of their mom's prayers.

David and I found it works best to start simply and pray for short periods of time as a couple. When we got married, I was the one who was uncomfortable praying aloud. So David was wise. He didn't push. Sometimes we prayed just a few sentences. Or, thank-you prayers are always a good place to begin.

Gradually, we found that bringing the Bible into our prayer time was valuable. When our children were old enough to join in our prayers, we'd have a brief family time together on Saturday nights. Perhaps we'd share a story or a verse that was speaking to us. We tried to find promises from the Bible that applied directly to whatever problems we were facing.

For several years, our family hoped together for a third baby. The children prayed faithfully for a little brother or sister. David and I had walked through infertility twice before and we weren't growing any younger. I was getting weary. So I kept praying to the Lord to please honor the persistent prayers of these two little children. Finally, when Bethany was nine and DB was nearly six, we learned that little Michael was on the way. What a party we had when we got the news! And what joy it gave us as parents to see our children rejoice over the answer to their prayers.

We also explored practical ways to make the Bible come alive. David was famous for getting the kids to act out a Bible story, and I would find ways to set Bible verses to song. Our now-grown kids still remember some of my silly tunes. We wove truth into daily life. The Bible encourages us to talk with our children about God's Word when we "sit at home and when you walk along the road, when you lie down and when you get up" (Deuteronomy 6:7). As we were coming and going, I would weave simple Bible verses into our conversations. Or David would use daily life to make a biblical point. You can see why it's important for us to stay well-fed from God's Word ourselves so we're ready when the teachable moments occur. We learned that the faith was "caught" as well as taught.

As our family did life together, we would also share our own faith stories, our answered prayers, our hopes and dreams. And our hearts. Above all, David and I simply wanted our children to realize that Jesus was real. We acknowledged His presence. Without being cheesy or preachy about it, we wanted them to honor Jesus as the King of our home.

Work Hard

Earlier I mentioned that David played basketball for the legendary coach Dean Smith.[3] After his sophomore year of mostly sitting on the bench, he yearned for more playing time. He approached Coach

Smith one afternoon, hoping to win his favor—and more minutes in the game. "Coach, how can I help the team?" David asked. To which Smith simply replied, "David, if you want more playing time, become a better player."

So that summer, David played pick-up games at the city park, toughened up under the basket, and ran mile after mile. He came back to Chapel Hill to begin his junior year in the best shape of his life. His hard work paid off—he got significantly more playing time.

Honor is about respect and esteem. Nobility. Honesty. It's also about hard work. Work is a gift from God. We honor Him by giving our best effort. By being faithful in the small things "Whatever you do," Paul wrote in Colossians 3:23, "work at it with all your heart, as working for the Lord" rather than for men.

We taught our children that all honest work is honorable—whether it's working at a grocery store, waiting on tables, weekly chores, or even folding laundry. Work is noble and has honor if we do our best. Sometimes I would point out the people in our daily path who appeared to be "working with all their heart," like the guy who loaded up our groceries one day with an especially cheerful attitude. Or the waitress who did an especially good job with our large order.

David and I share the belief that hard work is vastly underrated in today's world. We talk about the importance of big dreams. But without plenty of hard work, they remain just dreams. Author Gary Smalley gives this bit of advice to parents, which I took to heart: Helping your children find their gifts and talents is just part of the equation. Children know how to dream. What doesn't come quite so naturally is the willingness to stick to a goal. Practice in any endeavor is hard work, especially at first. So when a child commits to an activity, Smalley encourages parents to help him or her stick with it—at least for a mutually agreed upon length of time.[4]

David and I helped our kids experiment until they found

something they loved and were good at. Then we'd provide structure and discipline to help them stick with it until their efforts brought at least a measure of success.

Our children loved sports. But at different times, each would have chosen to skip out on practice, especially when early morning workouts became part of their routine. That's when our role as parents was to provide that little extra push they lacked to get up early. As they got older and developed a passion for their dreams, their own self-discipline kicked in with a fierce determination.

Dreams energize effort. And small but faithful habits can help accomplish big dreams. I shared earlier that I believe that a child's God-given dreams can have world-changing impact. In a commencement address, Navy admiral and former SEAL William H. McRaven challenged graduates at the University of Texas at Austin to dare to change their world:

> Changing the world can happen anywhere and anyone can do it...But change starts with small actions. Every morning we were required to make our bed to perfection. It seemed a little ridiculous at the time, particularly in light of the fact that we were aspiring to be real warriors, tough battle-hardened SEALs—but the wisdom of this simple act has been proven to me many times over. If you make your bed every morning you will have accomplished the first task of the day. It will give you a small sense of pride and it will encourage you to do another task and another and another. By the end of the day, that one task completed will have turned into many tasks completed. Making your bed will also reinforce the fact that little things in life matter.[5]

The admiral's final word of advice to the graduates? "If you want to change the world, start off by making your bed."

Enjoy God's Grace

The music blared loud and the children laughed as they did their own little self-styled dance moves to the popular contemporary Christian tune "Saddle Up Your Horses." Twenty years have come and gone, and yet I still smile when I remember their boundless enthusiasm. Every now and then, a lively Motown tune would also ripple through our house. Along with great worship music, life in our home included the likes of Smokey Robinson, the Jackson Five, and Stevie Wonder. But what the kids really loved was the laughter and celebration that came with the music. That, and lots of joy.

When we honor God and truly understand grace—His unmerited love and favor—joy naturally becomes part of the climate of our home. Grace is unbelievably good news. What a relief to realize we don't have to earn God's favor through adherence to rules and regulations. And once we've accepted Jesus as our Lord and Savior, nothing can ever "separate us from the love of God."[6]

Even so, I never assumed our children would simply absorb our faith. After all, I myself had wandered away from God as a young teen. But as Ruth Bell Graham beautifully shares in *Prodigals and Those Who Love Them*,[7] some kids just have to find their faith for themselves. She shares inspiring stories of several strong Christian leaders, including their own son Franklin Graham, who had wandered from the faith and come home again. Thank goodness, I had parents who, like Ruth Graham, prayed for me and patiently waited while I was on my search.

David and I hoped to win our children to the gospel, so our goal was to make it *winsome*. When we honor God, we'll naturally want to tell our children about His wonderful works. That's called glorifying Him, or giving Him a good reputation. *Glorify* is simply another word for honor.

We let the kids in on the things God was doing in our lives. And we hoped they'd let us in on what He was doing in theirs. We wanted them to "like" God as well as love Him. "Man's chief end," according to the Westminster catechism,[8] "is to glorify God, and to enjoy Him forever." Think about that for a minute. We're to *enjoy* God!

As I shared earlier, last Father's Day, I asked our three grownup kids to write out a few lines telling why they were thankful for their dad. A thankful heart, I've learned, is kind of a "superfood" when it comes to honoring my husband.

Their responses touched my heart—not only do our kids love and appreciate their dad, it appears they've also grasped grace. I noticed that David still keeps the card beside his chair. "You are an amazing father, role model, and friend," DB wrote. "I pray that one day I can be half of the man that you are. I look forward to moving back to Charlotte and getting to spend more time together!" Michael added, "I strive to emulate your actions and impact people's hearts the way you do. Thank you for always encouraging me and challenging me to be a better man." Bethany's wrote, "Daddy, you taught me about grace. You helped me not take life so seriously. You taught me joy and laughter. To dance. To sing. To feel deeply. To love. To give grace. To forgive."

David and I are flawed parents who have made lots of mistakes. And our children are certainly not perfect. David likes to say that all families are in some way dysfunctional because of the fall. That's why we need lots of grace, and that's why we did what we could to create a home where honor is present, thanksgiving flows freely, and "grace is in place."

Share a Cup of Water with the Thirsty

The conversation with my friend started out casually enough over dinner one night. But I have to tell you that 25 years later, it still stands out as a turning point in how I viewed God's purpose for our family. This friend was someone I didn't know very well, but I admired the way she was raising her family. She and I talked honestly about the challenges of raising kids in today's world.

I remarked that my life was very different than it had been in my earlier years when I was far from God. "I can't believe that my whole world now is Christian," I said. "I have a Christian pediatrician, a Christian dentist, even my hairdresser loves Jesus. Plus, I can't think of a single non-Christian friend...Just how did my world get so safe?" I wondered aloud. She paused and looked at me and said without a trace of apology, "Oh, that's my world too. I've worked very hard to get it that way, and I plan to keep it that way."

I was taken aback. *Something's wrong here,* I thought to myself. What has happened to our call to reach the lost? My epiphany came gradually. Over the days and weeks that followed, I sensed God nudging me to reach out to our neighbors. We enrolled Bethany in our neighborhood school. David and I started a small-group Bible study in our home for parents of several of her classmates. Most were still searching and had lots of questions.

More and more, David and I began to turn our eyes outward to the broken world around us, taking our family with us whenever possible. We were still protective of where the kids were, who they were with, what they watched. So this meant their friends were often at our home. But I sensed that teaching our kids to hear God's voice for themselves was their best protection. Our family continued to be my highest calling. But I now saw our home as a way to engage the world, a place where honor and grace would spill over to those around us.

David and I noticed that as they got older, the children rose to the challenge in their own way and among their own friends. DB walked tall as a spiritual leader among his basketball teammates, giving witness to his faith by the way he lived his life. Seems he was always ready with an encouraging word or a listening ear. Michael often gravitates to friends who are searching. He called the other day to tell me that he had encouraged a fellow swimmer to read *Mere Christianity*, the same book that had led me to faith. Bethany was exuberant when a volleyball teammate from high school, whom she has been quietly loving all these years, recently accepted Jesus. Her beautiful friend, who happens to be Jewish, now knows Yeshua as her Messiah. "Daddy Chaddy," as she calls David, and I were overjoyed.

Jesus said words that should arrest us. He tells us that whatever we do for the least and the lost, "you did for me" (Matthew 25:40). We're to go out and look for the lost sheep. And we're to notice the ones around us who are thirsty. Perhaps honor is like a cup of cold water to a world choking on its own disgrace.

God's Ways Work

I once taught waterskiing at a summer camp on the North Carolina coast. In order to take the required Coast Guard test, we had to learn the maritime "rules of the road," as boat navigators like to call them. We also had to be able to identify channel markers alerting us to dangers such as shallow water and hidden objects. Following a few basic rules can make all the difference between smooth sailing and disaster—and sometimes between life and death.

While reflecting on ways to honor my husband, it dawned on me that the simple behaviors that go hand in hand with honor are kind of like God's "channel markers" for my marriage. By treating David with honor and respect, guarding my thoughts and words, believing the best about him, building him up as the spiritual leader of our home, and staying strong in my own walk with the Lord, I'm protected from hidden dangers and obstacles that could threaten our marriage.

Honor is such a lofty theme—I had been wracking my brain for a couple of days trying to think of a fitting way to close this book, when my cell phone suddenly rang. It was Martha, our dear friend who helped us start the Carpenter's Class so long ago. Martha and I hadn't talked in quite some time, but at 87, she is as vibrant as ever.

"Did you hear the news?" she asked excitedly. Martha went on to tell me that the daughter of some of our former classmates had just gotten married over the weekend. More than 20 Carpenter's Class members had traveled from far and wide across the country to attend the wedding. "You'd be so proud of the kids," as she still refers to us. The group had done very well, she said. Many were influential Christian leaders in their churches and communities. Best of all, they'd built strong marriages. And they're leaving behind their own legacy of faithful families.

In her follow-up email to me the next day, Martha wrote, "I don't think you and David realize the impact your 15-month time here had on so many lives. I consider my Carpenter Class experience as one of the major blessings of my life. Love to you both. Martha."

I thought back to those humble beginnings with the Carpenter's Class. With just three weeks of marriage under our belt, all we had to offer was a sincere belief in God's Word—that, and high hopes for our marriage. I also remembered about our Bible study group of wives—our little team of *ezers*—who were committed to honoring and respecting our husbands. We were intent upon following God's ways. Our simple belief was that if we took time to pray, read God's Word, and worship together, our marriages would not only make it, they would thrive. It was as if our laboratory experiment in marriage had come full circle—nearly 40 years later.

But what hit me most is simply this: God's ways work. Honoring my husband, becoming his *ezer*, his rock of support—this was God's idea from the very beginning. I know from experience that His rules of the road for marriage, and for all of life, can be trusted.

But the topic of honor has especially captured my interest. Through conversations with friends about how they honor their husbands, I've come to realize I've only scratched the surface. Finding ways to show honor may very well be one of the most important, and yet most often overlooked, aspects of marriage.

There's a curious thing about honor: You don't have to feel it to give it. You don't have to agree with or even like a person to show them honor. That's why honor can be a first step for a marriage in trouble. When you honor your husband, you can bring health to a hurting marriage or make a good one better.

I've noticed that being more intentional to honor David has breathed some fresh life into our already-strong marriage. So I'll keep practicing. And I plan to continue asking women, "How do you honor your husband?" I think we'd agree that honor is long forgotten in today's world. So I challenge you to keep the conversation about honor going. Let's take God at His Word and treat our husbands with honor and respect. Let's fill our homes with a culture of honor. And let's dare to shine bright in a world that's desperate for a better way to do marriage.

EPILOGUE:

Keep Calm and Carry On

WHEN PEOPLE MEET MY nearly 90-year-old dad, they often ask me, "What's his secret?" "How does your dad look so young and stay so sharp?" Daddy would be the first to tell you that part of his secret is that he has a great wife. He's been married to my mom for more 60 years.

My mother has been nearly bedridden for the last ten or so of those years. A ruptured appendix and complications from a subsequent surgery robbed the robust grandmother of her ability to walk. Some of her ability to think and talk has faded. But enough of her razor-sharp mind is still there that conversation is possible, though difficult. Daddy insists upon caring for her at home with the assistance of nurses' aides, who help him with wheelchair transfers and daily care.

If you asked them, Mom and Dad would each say they "married up." Mom would always tell us three girls how lucky she was to find Daddy. And Dad said he was just glad his "turn in line" with the other young men who wanted to date Mom finally came. To which Mom would answer back, "Well I was hoping you would ask me out!" Just the other day, Dad looked at my mom, lying in the bed after he had just brushed her hair, and said to me, "Doesn't she look pretty?"

Few could imagine the daunting challenges Mom and Dad now face on a daily basis just to live at home. Dad does the grocery shopping, the cooking, the cleaning, the laundry. There are medical procedures Dad performs each day. Catheters, baths, diapers. There have been occasional trips to the emergency room or hospitalization because of infections. Dad's caregiver role began after Mom's appendix ruptured ten years ago. Even then, he managed the daily cleaning of Mom's open abdominal wound for weeks after her emergency surgery. Dad's days are harder when his bad back flares up.

In good times and hard times, Mom and Dad have honored their wedding vows. That in itself is a legacy of honor, which they have passed on to David and me, to our children, and their children. But there is much more.

How Mom Honored Dad

Since this is a book on how to honor your husband, I've spent time reflecting on specific ways I remember Mom honoring Dad over the years. Looking back, I can see some of the reasons their marriage has remained strong. Sometimes when we're in the middle of daily life as it's happening, we don't fully realize the truly heroic nature of the people right in front of us. It all seems normal at the time. So it's been special for me to take a look back at the life my parents lived and the legacy they left me. As I reflect, I feel enormous gratitude for their sacrifices that paved the way for the life I have today.

We've been talking about the importance of how to honor your husband in marriage. So it has helped me to think back about Mom and Dad's life together with *honor* as my lens. How did Mom honor Dad? What are some ways they honored each other? And what kind of legacy have they left to those who come behind them?

During our growing-up years, Mom was Dad's helper in the best sense of the word. She was a true *ezer*. She was strong and kind. And she was his rock of support. I remember how Mom built Dad up. She believed in him.

Mom had stopped teaching school when the kids came—family was everything to her. She especially loved Dad's parents and his three sisters and their families. She even took an interest in Dad's sales force—"Daddy's men," as she called them—and sometimes we got together with their families.

Dad's job as a regional sales manager with a large company required quite a bit of travel. Mom never complained. She simply kept life going for her three daughters. But invariably, most of our life crises seemed to hit when Daddy was away. Like the time I tried to do a cannonball dive into three feet of water and didn't tuck quite fast enough, hitting my head on the bottom of the swimming pool. After Mom and I took a fast trip to the emergency room and 27 stitches later, Dad finally made it home.

Recently, when I asked Daddy to describe some ways Mom had honored him, he pointed back to that incident. "I never worried when I was traveling," he said. "Even when you cracked your head open, I could always count on your mom to handle things. She was always so calm."

Daddy's right. Mom honored him by her strong resolve and her ability to keep the family on track in his absence. The now widely popular World War II expression "Keep calm and carry on" was originally created to inspire the Brits to keep their courage during the war. And I think it describes my mom quite well.

Mom and Dad suffered two especially hard losses as a young couple. When I was about two, Mom delivered a baby girl who died shortly after she was born a few weeks premature. Today's neonatal technology could likely have saved the baby. I have no memories of this incident.

Tragically, the very same thing happened again when I was five.

This one I do remember. There were two of us kids now, my sister Susan and me. Mom went into premature labor again and delivered a baby—another girl who also died soon after birth. But Mom, just 28 at the time, somehow managed to keep life moving forward in our home. I know she had a deep faith, and I'm sure it was her faith and her courage that gave her the strength to persevere. She and Daddy kept hope alive, and two years later welcomed my youngest sister, Janice, whose name means "God's gracious gift," into our family.

I'm a mother myself now, and a grandmother. So when I look back at those times in my mother's life, I don't know how she kept going. She and Daddy had to be grieving. Yet I'm amazed at how little she allowed those terrible losses to impact our lives as children. By that I mean that she and my dad didn't retreat to fear or hold us back from a normal, active, and happy childhood. Mom kept moving forward for us—evidence, again, of her self-sacrificial nature and her servant's heart.

How They Honored Each Other

Mom was an only child and had always wanted to be part of a large family. So she especially loved Daddy's large family. And Daddy loved hers. They were a team. Family was their priority.

They also shared each other's interests, like a love of the outdoors. They enjoyed camping. Some of my favorite childhood memories— even into my teen years—are of our family camping trips every summer. To the beach, to the mountains. To historic sites such as Colonial Williamsburg and Kitty Hawk.

Mom and Dad both had keen minds. They loved good books and good movies, and made sure we had access to those things growing up. They appreciated education, patriotism, and the land. Our people were mostly a collection of educators, farmers, and those serving in the military. Being native Virginians, they especially loved all things Virginian.

Honor was present in so many ways in our home, though typical of their generation, they didn't flaunt it. I guess you could say Mom and Dad were good, solid, honorable people who came from a long line of good solid, honorable people. They had all had long-lasting marriages and were proud of their heritage. And they passed that legacy on to us.

TELLING OUR FAMILY STORIES

Daddy happens to be one of the few remaining World War II submarine veterans. He and my mom vividly remember the war—they don't take our freedoms for granted. So growing up, neither did we. One of the ways they helped us appreciate our heritage was to tell lots of stories—especially stories about our family. I grew up hearing about Daddy's submarine adventures in the South China Sea. And about rations and blackouts, or brave young friends who lost their lives in the war.

Mom and Dad were also proud of our family's long history in this country dating back to before the Revolutionary War. Captain Simon Hunt, from Daddy's mother's side, was one of the original 90 or so minutemen who fought the British in the famous battle on the Old North Bridge in Concord, Massachusetts. It was on that bridge that the "shot heard round the world" signaled the beginning of the Revolutionary War. Our youngest, Michael Hunt Chadwick, loved hearing his grandparents' stories of the Hunt family and his namesake.

Looking back over my life, I can also see how Mom and Dad's values quietly shaped my own. They grew up in the South back in the day before the Civil Rights movement had ushered in change. They didn't talk much about racism, but they lived a life that spoke volumes to me. I watched how they lived. To them, all people mattered. Everyone had worth. Everyone was equal. And all were welcome in our home. Black. White. Old money, new money, or no money. They treated everybody the same, and their simple, as well as honorable, example spoke louder than any sermon.

Get an Education

Education was a given in our home. Mom and Dad were both college graduates back in the day when that was not common. Mom had been the valedictorian of her small country high school, and Dad was a campus leader and played basketball at his high school, finishing early to go into the navy. He qualified for submarine school and left for his tour of duty, then returned after the war to go to college on the GI Bill.

Mom's mother, my Grandmother Eunice, taught first grade for about 50 years. Sometimes when I would run errands with her in their small town in southern Virginia, grown-ups would stop and say proudly to me that my grandmother had been their favorite teacher and the one who taught them how to read.

I found my grandmother fascinating. One of eight children, her parents had died when she was very young, back in the late 1800s. She left home at an early age and somehow managed to go to college and became a teacher. Then she hopped on a cross-country train trip going west and taught school in various places along the way.

She made her way to Montana and eventually to Pasadena, California, where she taught for a few years, even attending one of the very first Rose Parades. Then she hopped back on another train and made her way back across the country. She again stopped here and there to teach. I remember looking at photos of the time she rode by mule to the bottom of the Grand Canyon.

Finally, back in Virginia, my grandmother, at age 38, married my Granddaddy, a farmer. He had met the pretty young schoolteacher before her travels west, and I suppose he was holding out until her return. By this time, he was 48. They married and had my mom a year later—their only child.

My dad's mother, Grandmother Lois (the irony of a Eunice and a Lois will not be lost on some of you), was another special role model for me, and I adored her. Like my Grandmother Eunice, she also attended college back in the day when few women did and played on the very first women's basketball team at William & Mary College in Williamsburg, Virginia. So you see why getting an education was its own "code of honor" in our family. My parents thought of education as noble. Even a responsibility, along with duty, sacrifice, and honor.

No Matter What Comes Your Way, Finish Strong

Live a life of sacrifice and honor. Give yourself for the larger good. Put others before yourself. Don't give up. Family is worth it. No matter what comes your way, persevere. And always do the right thing. These were some of the messages my parents taught me by example over the years.

Mom and Dad believed in dreaming big and always encouraged our dreams. Through the years, nothing brought them more joy than to watch their children and grandchildren (and now great-grandchildren) shine.

But this last chapter of life is hard. Honor is now an uphill climb. For them, doing the right thing day after day requires endurance, faith, and sometimes a good sense of humor. I've watched their courageous battle and I agree with whoever said "Old age is not for sissies." I watch my mom's quiet and uncomplaining spirit even when she is in pain. And I see Daddy's cheerful attitude as he perseveres day after day.

"How do you do it, Dad?" I asked the other day. He just shrugged his shoulders and said matter-of-factly, "Your mom is worth it." I look at their life in the light of the meaning of the word *honor*—to show a person respect and esteem. To treat someone as though they have great worth. Honor by its very nature is strong, solid, and above all, enduring. I'd have to say Mom and Dad are living examples of honor and a testimony to its high cost—not something you hear much in our "it's all about me" culture.

Just the other day, Mom and Dad had an especially difficult morning that stretched Daddy to practically the end of his strength. Some days are harder than others. Later that day, Daddy quietly beamed as he told me about how Mom had looked at him that morning for a minute or so and then spoke these words with perfect clarity: "You are so patient. I am so proud of you."

Just a few simple words from his wife who doesn't talk so much anymore. And yet Daddy wore those words like they were a medal of honor. And if you think about it, I guess that's truly what they are.

Honor. A concept so simple even a child can grasp it. God set the bar low so that even the youngest and weakest among us can practice honor. But God has also set the bar high. People defend freedom, fight, and die for honor. Believers around the world honor Jesus by suffering for their faith. And honor inspires husbands and wives to love each other for a lifetime. In good times and in hard ones. Honor guards our marriages and sets them on solid ground. No wonder it's so important in our homes. By teaching us to treat each other with honor, God has set before us the most noble and enduring way to live together—with a love that never dies. So that we can finish strong.

50 Ways to Leave Your Legacy

Alegacy is lasting. It takes lots of little gestures over time to leave a legacy. Many people today would rather have fame than honor. But fame is fleeting, while honor is solid. And it's much easier to grab fame than to create honor. So when you decide to create a culture of honor in your home, you're going against the grain. But take heart. Your legacy will bless your children and future generations, along with a world that is yearning for something different.

I hope the following ideas will help you begin to practice honor within your family. Maybe they'll spur you on to come up with your own ideas. After all, every family is different. It's my prayer that as you create a climate of honor in your home, your husband and children will flourish and that the legacy you leave will be a lasting one.

Your legacy will also honor God and bless those around you. I agree with you in prayer that together we can start a movement of honor that will begin in our own marriages and families—then spill out of our hearts and our homes onto a thirsty and broken world.

1. Begin now to build simple traditions. Consider your family's age, stage, and interests. Experiment until you

find what works, and then keep at it! Remember, simple is sustainable.

2. "Pizza Family Home Night" was a Friday night ritual. It was our family's all-time favorite. Great movies. Pizza (easy to make, easier to order). Time alone with just our family. Can't beat that!

3. Find movies with the theme of honor. Our grown kids now have their own list of personal favorites. Heroes in movies can be a powerful way to make honor appealing. After a movie, talk with your kids about what they learned. To get your ideas rolling, here are a few of our kids' favorite movies as they got older: *Hoosiers, Seabiscuit, Remember the Titans, Chariots of Fire, Sound of Music, October Sky*, and many more.

4. Who are some of your personal heroes? Find ways to introduce your children to some of your role models and mentors—people who represent the ideal of honor. David took our children to his alma mater, the University of North Carolina, when they were young to watch the basketball team practice and meet his beloved Coach Dean Smith.

5. Read great books to your children—from the earliest age—that tell stories of faith, honor, courage, and other noble themes.

6. Help your children learn to show honor to the meaningful adults in their world, as well as to parents and grandparents.

7. Encourage your children to write letters to special family members on birthdays. For their grandparents' birthdays,

our kids listed the "top-ten favorite memories" of times with "Nannie and Grandaddy."

8. Ask family members and friends (even mentors, teachers, or youth pastors) to write a letter encouraging your child's hopes and dreams. We did this on thirteenth and sixteenth birthdays. Put the letters in a scrapbook.

9. Honor accomplishments; celebrate achievements.

10. Celebrate big and little events. We had a "You Are Special Today" meal plate. Now a classic, the bright red pottery versions are available online.

11. Celebrate little milestones in character. Did a child overcome a fear? We used to call that "conquering a fret fly." A great reason to go out for frozen yogurt!

12. Recognize and affirm your child's honorable behavior. Sometimes a smile or a hug is all that's needed. "Gotcha being good" as one friend calls it. Did a child show courage? Take up for a weaker kid? Demonstrate creativity by doing things differently than everyone else?

13. When a child was honest about a wrongdoing, we would sometimes lessen (but not erase) the penalty.

14. Affirm a cheerful attitude, especially if your child remains cheerful when things aren't going their way. The word *cheer* comes from the same root as the word *courage*.

15. Collect spiritual momentos to remind your family of God's work in their lives.

16. Make a "God Box." I found a lovely box that's about two feet in diameter. Spiritual momentos, Bible verses that have special meaning, stories of answered prayers all go into the God Box.

17. Now and then, share a few items from the God Box as reminders that God is always at work—even when we can't see it at the time.

18. Have weekly family prayer times with a brief Bible message. Ours were on Saturday nights. Ask the children for their prayer needs and give thanks for answered prayers.

19. Pray prayers of thanks at bedtime. A thankful heart is an honorable heart. Each night when they put their three-year-old daughter to bed, a couple I know takes turns sharing things in their day for which they are thankful. This builds sweet memories with their daughter—and it ends the day on a note of gratitude.

20. Help your children explore ways to honor God with their money. When they were very young, we gave each child ten dimes for their allowance. The first dime went into the offering plate, the second into a savings jar. The rest could be spent or saved for something special to buy. Dimes don't go far these days, but you get the point.

21. Have a prayer trigger for each child, as well as one for you and your husband, to remind you to pray throughout the day.

22. Memorize the fifth commandment together when your children are young. Remind them that God gave that special commandment just to them, and it even comes with a promise: "Honor your father and mother"— which is the first commandment with a promise—"so that it may go well with you and that you may enjoy long life on the earth" (Ephesians 6:1-3).

23. Stress respectful behaviors. Manners matter. Eye contact,

strong handshake, "Yes m'am" and "Yes sir" (remember, we're from the South), or at least a polite yes or no is important.

24. Encourage "good enough" table manners. I'd tease our kids: "Make sure your manners are 'good enough' so you're ready to eat dinner with the Queen of England if you're ever invited."

25. Make sure your kids know how to work hard. Clean a bathroom, make breakfast, do laundry. Later, they will thank you.

26. Stress personal responsibility. Find a system for family chores and some kind of allowance that works best for you.

27. Pray with your children for their friends, especially those who are spiritually seeking. Let your child know you will be continually praying for their friend.

28. Keep what your children share with you about their friends confidential. Enough said.

29. Remind your kids when they are teenagers that independence is an illusion until they are paying their own bills. (This can be a good comeback when they tell you that "So-and-so has more independence than I do.")

30. Have curfews. We did. "Nothing good happens after midnight," we'd always say.

31. Be alert for teachable moments, especially when riding in the car with your children. Our kids seemed to ask so many questions about God while in our van that I nicknamed our drive time "e-van-gelism." As I recall, the van is also where they asked most of their questions about

sex. Maybe they felt free to open up during our rides since I had to keep my eyes on the road.

32. Take seriously your responsibility to disciple your children. Find ways to help them learn the Bible. GT and the Halo Express series was our favorite Bible memory tool.

33. Remind your children about the day they accepted Jesus into their heart. This advice came from a wise children's worker who encouraged me never to take lightly those early decisions of faith—no matter how young the child was when he or she received Christ.

34. Because of the advice in #33, I was mindful to point out specific details about our children's decisions of faith. For example, I used to tell Bethany the story of how she accepted Jesus when she was not quite three while we were riding in the car at "just this spot in the road."

35. Attend a strong church that teaches God's Word. We included the children in our regular worship services as early as possible.

36. Text your teenage (and even adult) kids a Bible verse that the Lord puts on your heart each morning. My friend Kelly (mom to DB's lovely bride, Jessie) came up with this idea. She calls this her "Mom's Verse of the Day" (MVOD). Even her grown kids will remind her if she forgets to send the MVOD.

37. Find a prayer partner—like my friend Beth—who is always alert and ready to pray on a moment's notice. We simply send a POD (prayer on demand), and sometimes a verse of Scripture via text. We trust God to do the rest.

38. Instead of exchanging Christmas gifts with a friend, here's an idea: Go out for coffee. Select a Bible verse together and commit to praying that verse for each other's children for next year as your Christmas "gift" to each other. For one whole year, a friend and I prayed this promise from Psalm 144:12 for our kids: "Then our sons in their youth will be like well-nurtured plants, and our daughters will be like pillars carved to adorn a palace."

39. Tell your family stories of faith to remind your children of their spiritual heritage.

40. Encourage the grandparents to tell their stories.

41. Tell your children how they were named.

42. What is your heritage? All families have ancestors who were heroes or you wouldn't be here. Who are some of yours? Share this information with your kids.

43. Share your testimony of faith with your children. Tell them what God is doing in your life today.

44. Encourage your children's dreams. Remind them that nothing is too hard for God.

45. Help your children persist through the hard times and places—especially when working toward a goal.

46. Explore missions opportunities in your church and community.

47. Consider sponsoring a child in another country. Let your children contribute to the monthly cost.

48. Donate to a missions cause, or better yet, go on a family missions trip.

49. Select special giving projects for Christmas. We would let the children help us decide where the family Christmas offering would be designated.

50. Don't travel this "journey" alone. Find other moms and create a culture of honor together. Pray together for your family's legacy to be a lasting one that blesses future generations.

50 Ways You Can Begin to Honor Your Husband Right Now

To honor my husband means to treat him with respect and admiration. To say, "You're special and have great worth in my eyes." Little gestures go a long way. Take what works, toss out what doesn't, and get creative with ideas of your own!

1. Decide that your husband will be your priority—not just an add-on to your busy life.

2. Be his best friend. Become a better listener.

3. Go out for coffee or a date night. Listen to your husband. What are his dreams?

4. Ask God to show you specifically how to honor your husband. Study him. Watch what makes him feel honored. It's different for each husband. Be creative.

5. Pray for God to reveal ways you may be dishonoring your husband—maybe you're doing this without even knowing it.

6. Explore specific ways to lighten his workload and maximize his time at home.

7. Respond to his sense of humor. Find ways to laugh—often.

8. Make a list of the qualities that drew you to your husband when you first met him. Share with him a few items from the list—perhaps in a Father's Day or birthday card.

9. Encourage your children (of any age—even your grown kids) to write down a few things they are thankful for about their dad. Print these and put them in a card.

10. Find one thing to thank your husband for each day— gratitude is like the "superfood" of honor.

11. Go to bed at the same time whenever possible.

12. Find a hobby or activity you can do together—especially something outdoors.

13. Greet your husband warmly when he comes home. Stop what you're doing. Look him in the eye. Give him a smile, or even better, a kiss.

14. Ask your husband, "Is there one thing I can pray for you today?" It helps to be specific. Pray. Check in later with him for an update.

15. Find a Bible promise that relates to his situation. Pray that promise for him or text him the verse.

16. Watch and learn from your friends who do a good job of honoring their husbands.

17. Be intentional to give your husband a few minutes of focused attention when he first gets home. One friend with small children confided that her "multitasker personality" would kick in. "I was trying to fold clothes, unload the dishwasher or do something 'productive'

while we talked." That has changed, however. "Now I'm trying to be fully present," she said.

18. Consider waking up together, if this is possible with you. My prayer partner has been married to her husband more than 40 years. She likes to wake up together with him and bring him coffee each morning.

19. Commit to growing in your own relationship with the Lord. Find a spiritual mentor if that would help you get motivated. When you are strong in the Lord, it will spill over into your marriage and family.

20. Thank your husband for what he brings to the home—for his hard work.

21. Let your husband know you are still attracted to him. Stay fit and keep looking nice—it's one more way to honor him.

22. Kidnap your husband for an overnighter. I would work with David's assistant to clear his calendar, hire a sitter, and find a nearby bed and breakfast. Even a short time away is replenishing.

23. Pray together.

24. Save some energy for your husband even if you have a hectic schedule. One friend and her husband are busy professionals with an empty nest. She reminds herself to give her best energy when they get time alone. I like the way she puts it: "I need to show up well."

25. Refuse to let social media dominate your home time.

26. Take a day off together each week. Maybe a weekly date night or breakfast together works better—be creative with time off together. The key is to do this regularly.

27. Begin now to research fun dates. If childcare is an issue, start a "babysitter fund." One of my friends has come up with a list of great little day trips all within an hour's drive from home.

28. Find a way to spend time reconnecting and relaxing at the end of the day—get the children to bed a little earlier.

29. Our kids are grown, so our favorite way to relax at the end of a long workday looks like this: Netflix and hot-air organic popcorn drizzled with warm coconut oil and sea salt. We share a dark chocolate bar. Yum!

30. Set your cell phone alarm to remind you to pray for your husband. Keep a prayer list, a journal, or a bulletin board. Have a prayer trigger that reminds you to pray for him. Pick one for yourself too. One friend prays when she folds clothes. Whatever works!

31. Pray for little problems (that he may not see) before they become big problems. Do not feel you have to always bring these to his attention.

32. Leave notes or text words of encouragement.

33. Speak encouraging words to your husband in front of others—especially the kids.

34. Share with your friends something you admire about your husband when he is *not* there.

35. Compliment your husband to his face. Sincere, specific compliments fill the tank of your marriage like nothing else.

36. Conflict happens. If you have something negative to say, "sandwich" it. Words of grace...then the truth...then more grace.

37. Remember: It's been said we need to hear ten comments of affirmation for every criticism.

38. Encourage your husband to dream big. Celebrate when he reaches a goal.

39. Recapture special memories in a gift. Our daughter-in-law had a quilt made from our son's athletic shirts.

40. Pray the B-L-E-S-S prayer for "his Body, or his physical health; his Labor, which is his job; his Emotional health; his Spiritual growth; and his Social relationships."

41. Find appealing ways to help your husband eat healthy—and exercise. Do *not* nag, but set an example. Or better, find a way to exercise together outdoors.

42. Resist the urge to constantly criticize or correct. Go on a "word fast" from critical words for a day. I've heard it said, "It's God's job to make our husband holy; it's our job to make him happy."

43. Refuse to take part in "husband bashing" with friends or associates.

44. Be mindful to honor your husband's reputation. One friend is transparent with close friends about disagreements in her marriage, but only when she is able to share how they worked it out. She's careful not to damage how her friends see her husband.

45. Honor your husband's parents, even when they are not present. You can show honor even if you don't always agree with them.

46. Find a specific verse of Scripture to inspire you to honor your husband. One wise friend decided to practice a different aspect of honoring her husband each day from

the following verse: "The wife [must see to it] that she respects and delights in her husband [that she notices him and prefers him and treats him with loving concern, treasuring him, honoring him, and holding him dear]" (Ephesians 5:33 AMP).

47. Encourage your husband's spiritual leadership— especially with your kids. Don't quench his enthusiasm or take over the spiritual leadership role. Especially if you have more Bible knowledge.

48. Attend church together regularly with your husband; take a class or be in a small Bible study group together.

49. Find a way to serve together. For example, work at a local homeless shelter. Or, how about a short-term missions trip?

50. Stay strong in your own relationship with God. Regular times of prayer, Bible study, and strong friends who will pray with and for you will all make a huge difference over the long haul.

Study Questions

1

First, Become Strong

What does it mean to honor someone?

In Genesis 2:18, the Hebrew word translated "helper" is *ezer*. What are some of the things that the biblical concept of *ezer* refer to?

In the chapter, it's stated that true strength requires humility. Why do you think this is the case?

As we abide in Christ, we are enabled in our role as our husband's *ezer*. Read John 15:1-5. What are some practical ways we can make abiding in Christ a daily reality in our lives?

2

Believe the Best

There are many ways that today's culture encourages women to dishonor their husbands. What are some examples of this? What are some ways Christian wives can counter this?

"Honor may be best expressed through words and deeds, but it begins in the mind." Do you agree with that statement? Why or why not? Read that statement again, then read Philippians 4:8. In relation to honoring your husband, what are some ways you can put Philippians 4:8 to work in your life?

A key aspect of honoring your husband is to guard your mind. What kinds of influences do you think you should guard against? What kinds of influences can you welcome?

As you seek to honor your husband, you'll find it helpful to write a gratitude list of things you appreciate about him. Start that list now, and add to it in the days ahead. Spend time in prayer, and ask God to help you be thankful each day for the things you write on your list.

3

Build Him Up

A key way to honor your husband is to let him lead. What are some ways a wife can inadvertently undermine her husband's leadership? What are some ways she can encourage his leadership?

Words can build up or tear down. What kinds of words would tear down a husband? What words would build him up? When it comes to speaking words of life to your husband, what are some ways you can improve?

Have the kids write down just two or three sentences about what they are thankful for in their dad. Print their words and put them in a card for your husband's birthday or Father's Day.

"There are times to say it, and times to pray it." What are some ways to know when it's better to pray about something than to say it?

Pick a day this week to go on a "word fast." At the end of the day, write down what you learned, and make a point of deliberately applying those lessons to your life.

4

Fight for Him

Can you think of one or two examples of *ezer* as an "early warning system," either from your own life or from another woman you respect?

Part of being your husband's *ezer* is having a warrior mentality that desires to protect your marriage. What are some of the "enemies" you face that desire to tear down your marriage?

What two weapons do we have to defend ourselves and our marriages?

"The single most important thing you can do to strengthen your marriage and honor your husband...[is to] pray for him." Why would praying for your husband be so important?

What are some ways you can be more intentional about praying for your husband? Commit to one or two of those ideas, and make them a daily practice—starting today.

Come up with a "prayer trigger" for your husband. Then take time today to specifically ask him how you can be praying for him, and make sure to pray those things daily.

5

Guard Your Home

What kind of environment do you desire to create in your home? With that in mind, what types of things can you do in your home to show support for your husband? Are there any ideas you could commit to making a reality this month?

To be a "keeper at home" speaks of guarding your home. What kinds of intruders can threaten the peace and safety of your home? What are some specific ways you can encourage peace within your home?

Fears or anxieties about the future can rob us of peace. What encouragement are we given in 1 Peter 5:7? What fears or anxieties are uppermost in your mind right now? Take time to lift them up to the Lord, and place them completely in His hands.

Disorder hurts families, while structure helps them. Why do you think structure is so important? What are some benefits of structure?

6

Lighten His Load

Dr. James Dobson has pointed out that overcommitment can hurt a marriage. Why do you think that is the case?

Do you and your husband have a weekly time of rest together—a time when you can replenish yourselves? If so, how has that time been beneficial? If not, what are some possible ways to create that time?

Ask your husband: What helps you to slow down and rest? (Even simple answers—like a nap—are fine!) What can you do to help make that down time and rest possible?

What does it mean to "learn to take a B"? What are some areas of your life in which you could "take a B" so that you can do better in more important obligations or priorities?

7

Dream Big Together

"Dreams can motivate us and guide us toward God's purposes for our lives." Can you think of examples when this has been true in your life? What are some of your husband's dreams? How can you show support for those dreams?

What is the "tall poppy syndrome"? What are some ways that we can inadvertently discourage our husband's or children's dreams? What are some specific prayers you can lift up to God to support your husband's or children's dreams?

Pages 116-121 list three benefits of dreaming together. What are they?

Our human tendency is to focus on our own dreams first. But what do passages like Romans 12:10 and Philippians 2:3-4 exhort us to do? How can your children and others around you benefit when you make an effort to share your husband's dreams?

8

Create a Culture of Honor

We all desire to be known, to be accepted by others. Sometimes we try to fulfill those longings by striving for fame or popularity. But why would honor be more desirable than fame or popularity?

One of the Ten Commandments instructs children to obey their parents. Why do you think this is so important for children to do? What are some long-term benefits they can experience from learning to show honor in the home?

What are some ways that you, as a mom, can help cultivate an atmosphere of honor in your home? As you answer this, think about the way family members talk, the role of teaching children responsibility around the house, and other such vehicles for instilling a culture of honor.

If you want to make the gospel attractive to your children, it helps to make it winsome. What are some ways you can do that?

Now that you've reached the end of this book, what one or two lessons about honoring your husband stood out the most to you, and why? Spend time in prayer about what you learned, and commit to being deliberate about showing honor to your husband on a consistent basis.

Notes

Whatever Happened to Honor?

1. *Merriam-Webster Collegiate Dictionary* (2015), s.v. "Honor," http://www.m-w.com.

2. You can read more about the impact of Coach Smith on my husband's life in his book *It's How You Play the Game* (Eugene, OR: Harvest House, 2015).

3. Marilynn Chadwick, "Dean Smith and dads: Are good dads back in style?," *The Charlotte Observer,* February 12, 2015.

Chapter 1—First, Become Strong

1. Marilynn Chadwick, *Sometimes He Whispers, Sometimes He Roars: Learning to Hear the Voice of God* (New York: Howard Books, 2012), p. 142.

2. Dr. Walter Bramson, "What is an Ezer?" February 20, 2013, http://drwalterbramson.com/what-is-an-azer.

Chapter 2—Believe the Best

1. Common English Bible (CEB).

2. Christine Wicker, "Essay: Christine Wicker asks why women are walking away from marriage," August 15, 2010, http://www.dallasnews.com/lifestyles/health-and-fitness/health/20100815-Essay-Christine-Wicker-asks-why-6851.ece.

3. Christine Wicker, "Essay."

4. Marcus Buckingham, *The One Thing You Need to Know* (New York: Free Press, 2005), pp. 18-22.

5. Matthew 5:22, 28.

6. John Burbridge, "Biscan: Never going to have another bad day," *The Times of Northwest Indiana,* March 11, 2015, pp. C1-C2.

7. Mounce Reverse-Interlinear™ New Testament at https://www.biblegateway.com/passage/?search=phil.+4%3A6-8&version=MOUNCE.

8. See at https://www.teknia.com/greek-dictionary/logizomai.

Chapter 3—Build Him Up

1. Titus 2:3-5 NASB—"Older women likewise are to be reverent in their behavior, not malicious gossips nor enslaved to much wine, teaching what is good, so that they may encourage the young women to love their husbands, to love their children, to be sensible, pure, workers at home, kind, being subject to their own husbands, so that the word of God will not be dishonored."

2. Here is the full list of instructions to husbands in Ephesians 5:25-33 NIV: "Husbands, love your wives, just as Christ loved the church and gave himself up for her to make her holy, cleansing her by the washing with water through the word, and to present her to himself as a radiant church, without stain or wrinkle or any other blemish, but holy and blameless. In this same way, husbands ought to love their wives as their own bodies. He who loves his wife loves himself. After all, no one ever hated their own body, but they feed and care for their body, just as Christ does the church—for we are members of his body. 'For this reason a man will leave his father and mother and be united with his wife, and the two will become one flesh.' This is a profound mystery—but I am talking about Christ and the church. However, each one of you also must love his wife as he loves himself, and the wife must respect her husband."

3. Fiona Macrae, "Sorry to interrupt, dear, but women really do talk more than men (13,000 words a day more to be precise)," *Daily Mail*, February 20, 2013, http://www.dailymail.co.uk/sciencetech/article-2281891/Women-really-talk-men-13-000-words-day-precise.html.

4. *Oxford Dictionaries* (2015), s.v. "slander," http://www.oxforddictionaries.com.

5. Spiros Zodhiates, ed., *Hebrew-Greek Key Word Study Bible*, NIV (Chattanooga, TN: AMG Publishers, 1996), p. 1599.

6. Galatians 5:22: "The fruit of the Spirit is love, joy, peace, forbearance, kindness, goodness, faithfulness, gentleness and self-control."

7. See at https://www.teknia.com/greek-dictionary/oikodomeo.

8. See at https://www.teknia.com/greek-dictionary/oikodomeo.

Chapter 4—Fight for Him

1. Romans 5:3-5 (NIV 1996 version).

2. 2 Corinthians 12:9.

3. Marilynn Chadwick, *Sometimes He Whispers, Sometimes He Roars: Learning to Hear the Voice of God* (New York: Howard Books, 2012).

4. Charles H. Spurgeon, *The Power of Prayer in a Believer's Life*, compiled and edited by Robert Hall (Lynn, WA: Emerald Books, 1993), p. 168.

5. Chadwick, *Sometimes He Whispers*, pp. 41-42.

6. See the entire Lord's Prayer in Matthew 6:10-13.

7. Joan Wright, *Up: Pursuing Significance in Leadership and Life* (Charlotte, NC: O'Sullivan Wright, 2012).

Chapter 5—Guard Your Home

1. From "The Declaration of Independence," adopted by the Continental Congress in Philadelphia, Pennsylvania on July 4, 1776.

2. See at https://en.wiktionary.org/wiki/a_man%27s_home_is_his_castle.

3. See at http://www.medieval-castle.com/architecture_design/medieval_castle_keeps.htm.

4. See at http://baptiststoday.org/walkers-round-trip-magnet/. Walker Knight, longtime editor of the Southern Baptist *Home Missions* magazine, wrote the widely quoted line which then President Jimmy Carter included in his Soviet Arms Limitation Treaty (SALT) talk: http://www.state.gov/t/isn/5195.htm.

5. Dr. Brene Brown, TED Talk, "The Power of Vulnerability," December 2010, https://www.ted.com/talks/brene_brown_on_vulnerability/transcript?language=en.

6. Matthew 10:26 esv.

7. Philippians 4:6 nkjv.

8. 2 Samuel 23:8-35.

9. Proverbs 31:25.

10. nlt.

11. I share a more detailed version of how I do my morning launch in my book *Sometimes He Whispers, Sometimes He Roars: Learning to Hear the Voice of God* (New York: Howard Books, 2012).

Chapter 6—Lighten His Load

1. Lawrence J. Epstein, "The Surprising Toll of Sleep Deprivation," *Newsweek*, June 18, 2010, http://www.newsweek.com/surprising-toll-sleep-deprivation-73183.

2. This quote is also popularly attributed to General George Patton.

3. Bill Hybels, "Reading Your Gauges," *Christianity Today*, Spring 1991, http://www.christianitytoday.com/le/1991/spring/9112032.html?start=6.

4. Dr. James Dobson, see at http://drjamesdobson.org/media/most-dangerous-threat-to-marriage.

5. Dr. James Dobson, *What Wives Wish Their Husbands Knew About Women* (Carol Stream, IL: Tyndale House, 2003), p. 54.

6. Exodus 20:8-11: "Remember the Sabbath day by keeping it holy. Six days you shall labor and do all your work, but the seventh day is a Sabbath to the LORD your God. On it you shall not do any work, neither you, nor your son or daughter, nor your male or female servant, nor your animals, nor any foreigner residing in your towns. For in six days the LORD made the heavens and the earth, the sea, and all that is in them, but he rested on the seventh day. Therefore the LORD blessed the Sabbath day and made it holy."

7. Mark 10:15.

8. Genesis 2:15.

9. Genesis 3:16 NKJV.

10. Genesis 3:19.

11. See Luke 12:18.

12. Greed is called idolatry in Colossians 3:5: "Put to death, therefore, whatever belongs to your earthly nature: sexual immorality, impurity, lust, evil desires, and greed, which is idolatry."

13. Exodus 20:17, which is the tenth commandment: "You shall not covet..."

14. Sandra Grimes and Jeanne Vertefeuille, *Circle of Treason: A CIA Account of Traitor Aldrich Ames and the Men He Betrayed* (Annapolis, MD: Naval Institute Press, 2013).

15. Wycliffe Bible.

16. Tim Keller, *Counterfeit Gods* (New York: Dutton, 2009).

17. 1 Timothy 6:17.

18. Isaiah 58:10.

19. See Hebrews 4:10.

Chapter 7—Dream Big Together

1. SIM (Serving in Mission) is an international missions organization that has its US headquarters located near Charlotte, North Carolina. SIM has been sending missionaries all over the world since the late 1800s. It began as a union of several organizations, including Sudan Interior Mission, and has had the longest active Christian witness in Sudan's history. You can learn more at their website http://www.sim.org/.

2. Romans 12:10.

3. Ephesians 5:25; 5:33; 5:21.

4. See Proverbs 27:17.

Chapter 8—Create a Culture of Honor

1. *Merriam-Webster Collegiate Dictionary* (2015), s.v. "Fame," http://www.m-w.com.

2. Dr. David Stoop, "The Couple that Prays Together," *Marriage & Family Matters*, August 6, 2012, http://drstoop.com/the-couple-that-prays-together/.

3. David Chadwick, *It's How You Play the Game* (Eugene, OR: Harvest House, 2015).

4. Gary Smalley, *The Key to Your Child's Heart* (Nashville, TN: Thomas Nelson, 1992), p. 155.

5. Admiral William H. McRaven, commencement speech given May 2014 at the University of Texas at Austin, https://www.youtube.com/watch?v=pxBQLFLei70.

6. Romans 8:38-39.

7. Ruth Bell Graham, *Prodigals and Those Who Love Them* (Grand Rapids, MI: Baker, 1991).

8. Westminster Shorter Catechism.

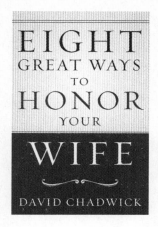

To learn more about Harvest House books and
to read sample chapters, visit our website:

www.harvesthousepublishers.com

HARVEST HOUSE PUBLISHERS
EUGENE, OREGON